INSTANT
PHILOSOPHY

T0160340

THIS IS A WELBECK BOOK

First published in 2021 by Welbeck,
an imprint of Welbeck Non-Fiction Limited,
part of the Welbeck Publishing Group
20 Mortimer Street
London W1T 3JW

Design © Welbeck Non-Fiction Limited 2021
Text copyright © Welbeck Non-Fiction Limited 2021

A CIP catalogue for this book is available from the British Library.

ISBN 978-1-78739-420-9

Printed in Dubai

10 9 8 7 6 5 4 3 2 1

The images in this publication are reproduced from thenounproject.com with the exception of the
following pages 13 Public Domain, 21 Lainspiratriz/Shutterstock, 22 Morphart Creation/Shutterstock,
23 Delcarmat/Shutterstock, 25 Macrovector/Shutterstock, 37 Matrioshka/Shutterstock, 44 Gabagool
via Wikimedia Commons, 52 CRStocker/Shutterstock, 55 Proskurina Yuliya/Shutterstock, 84
Alexander_P/Shutterstock, 164 Artbesouro/Shutterstock

INSTANT
PHILOSOPHY

KEY THINKERS, THEORIES, CONCEPTS AND DEVELOPMENTS EXPLAINED ON A SINGLE PAGE

GARETH SOUTHWELL

WELBECK

CONTENTS

EARLY MODERN PHILOSOPHY

LATER MODERN PHILOSOPHY

INTRODUCTION

Philosophy is difficult to define – in fact, perhaps the most we can agree on is that it began some two and a half millennia ago in Ancient Greece. During this period, it has developed out of or walked alongside numerous other concerns and disciplines, and yet has remained distinct from them. So, if you were to sign up to a philosophy class tomorrow, although you might discuss the existence of God, the nature of the mind, or the perfect system of governance, you would not strictly speaking be doing theology, psychology, or politics.

What makes philosophy independent, even where it touches on topics that belong to other disciplines, is the type of answers it seeks. Put simply, the deeper and more profound the nature of the questions it asks, the more likely we are to be doing philosophy. A physicist may ask *how* the universe began, but perhaps not *why*, or even what significance that holds for human existence. A psychologist may seek to understand how the mind works, but is unlikely to get grant funding to explore the question of how we can know whether other minds are like ours (assuming an experiment could settle that question anyway). Of course, there is some overlap between philosophy and other disciplines, and I don't mean to suggest that there are firm subject boundaries that should (or could) be observed. In fact, the history of philosophy contains numerous points where philosophers have been evicted from a form of enquiry that they themselves began (physics and psychology being two good examples). I merely want to point out that there is a sense in which what philosophy aims at is different.

The best way to understand this difference, of course, is to dive in – which is where *Instant Philosophy* comes in. Of course, I am under no illusion that a book such as this can convey the full range of depth and detail required to give you a good understanding of philosophy – what single book could? Rather, it seeks to provide an accessible, engaging, and occasionally humorous account of some of philosophy's central theories, concepts, movements, and thinkers. As such, I hope you find things that catch your interest, and intrigue you enough to follow them up (for this purpose, there is a Further Reading section at the end, together with a brief glossary). Along the way, as well as getting a handle on the things philosophers have argued about (and in many cases still do), you should start to get a better feel for what philosophy is – better than I can convey in this brief introduction, anyway!

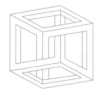

Instant Philosophy takes a broadly historical approach to the subject – from Ancient Greece to the present day – a survey that passes through the main regions of philosophy: metaphysics (the fundamental nature of reality, and what exists), epistemology (the theory of knowledge – what we can know and how; the role of certainty), political philosophy (the best form of government; freedom of the individual; legitimacy of authority), ethics (the nature of goodness; why we should be good; justifying our actions), aesthetics (the philosophy of art – the nature of beauty; art and truth), the philosophy of mind (mind's relation to the body; the nature of consciousness), philosophy of religion (arguments for the existence of God; the problem of evil), and philosophy of science (the nature of scientific theory; how we can guarantee scientific truth). This is not a strict division – often topics will cross over boundaries, or might be better categorized under a heading not included here – but I have (I hope forgivably) kept categories to a minimum for the sake of simplicity. The same thing applies to the association of philosophers with certain "schools", which are merely intended as a sign of the philosopher's general approach, not an indication of strict membership of any club.

It should also be noted that what is covered here – with some obvious exceptions – is mainly *Western* philosophy. This is not to downplay the importance of other traditions, but merely to explore those things that most would consider "philosophy" (and might think it odd if they did not find them included). This may not please everyone, but the topics and thinkers dealt with here are not meant to be definitive – merely, as I say, a jumping-off point for further investigation, and there should be sufficient diversity to at least indicate where competing notions of what philosophy is and does may be found.

Gareth Southwell

NATURAL PHILOSOPHY

The Western philosophical tradition began in and around Ancient Greece in the sixth to fifth century BC, and is often traced back to Thales.

THE BIRTHPLACE OF PHILOSOPHY

Thales was the first of a group of "**natural philosophers**" whose enquiries mark the point at which **explanations for the world and everything in it** were sought more and more in **human** or **natural terms**, through **logic and mathematics**, rather than **religion or mythology**. These pioneers seem to have been especially concerned with the *arche* (the **first principle or element of the natural world**), and for that reason their area of interest was termed "**natural philosophy**", a term which for the next two millennia would designate what we now simply call "**science**".

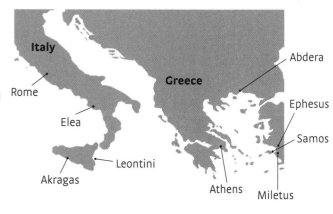

THE PRE-SOCRATICS

These early philosophers are now known more broadly as *Pre-Socratics* because they existed either before the **Greek philosopher Socrates**, or followed a **distinct tradition** from him, more interested in the **physical world** than in **ethics** or other **philosophical questions.**

Notable Pre-Socratics

Thales (Miletus), c.624–c.548 BC
Anaximander (Miletus), c.610–c.546 BC
Anaximenes (Miletus), c.586–c.526 BC
Pythagoras (Samos), c.570–c.495 BC
Xenophanes (Ephesus), c.570–c.475 BC
Heraclitus (Ephesus), c.535–c.475 BC
Parmenides (Elea), c.515–c.440 BC
Protagoras (Abdera), c.490–c.420 BC
Zeno (Elea), c.490–c.430 BC
Gorgias (Leontini), c.483–c.375 BC
Empedocles (Akragas), c.494–c.434 BC
Democritus (Abdera), c.460–c.370 BC

NAME THALES

DATES 624–548 BC

NATIONALITY GREEK (MILETUS)

SCHOOL PRE-SOCRATIC (MILESIAN)

MAIN WORKS NO WRITINGS SURVIVE

KEY CONTRIBUTIONS METAPHYSICS

THALES

Thales himself thought that the *arche* was **water**, for it could take **solid**, **liquid**, or **gaseous** form. His pupil **Anaximander** argued that it was something more **indefinable** and **abstract**; what he termed the *apeiron* ("**indefinite**" or "**boundless**"). His pupil, **Anaximenes**, thought the *arche* was **air**, because like it, **everything in the world** was in **constant motion**. **Heraclitus** thought it was **fire**, because its **fundamental nature was change**. But it is to **Empedocles** that we owe the idea that would **dominate later philosophy and science** for centuries, and seems almost a **synthesis of previous theories**: that **matter** in fact consists of **four elements**: **earth**, **air**, **fire**, and **water**.

DAOISM

Laozi was an ancient Chinese sage who preached that the true nature of reality could not be understood through words and labels but only through mindful being.

 NAME LAOZI

 DATES FL. C. SIXTH CENTURY BC

 NATIONALITY CHINESE

 SCHOOL DAOISM

 MAIN WORKS *THE DAO DE JING*

 KEY CONTRIBUTIONS EPISTEMOLOGY, METAPHYSICS, ETHICS

THE DAO

Little is known of Laozi, and it has been proposed that his **sole work** – the **Dao De Jing** (**The Book of the Way and of Virtue**) – may be a **collation** of the **sayings** of **various Chinese sages**. Its main subject is the **Dao** (**The Way**). This is **not a simple concept to describe**, for it is at once a **force that pervades Nature**, the **flow of events**, and an **ideal state of being**.

INTELLECTUALIZATION

Yet the **purpose** of Daoism is **not simply to mystify**, but to attempt to **release the hold** that **rational concepts** have on our **experience of reality**. As such, Daoism is more concerned with **realizing a state of being** than with **acquisition of intellectual knowledge**. And it is only through **giving up** the **desire to define** and "**know**" (so dear to **Western philosophy**), by adopting an attitude of **spontaneous mindfulness in harmony with Nature**, that we can **"understand" reality** in the **fullest sense**.

INEFFABLE

However, it is this **ineffable quality** that provides a clue as to the **Dao's nature** and how it may be **embodied**. Dao is an **ultimate reality** that **resists labels** and **conceptualization**. As the *Dao De Ching* states, **if we could describe the Dao**, then that **would not be the real Dao**. In this **resistance to definitions**, **Daoism** has much in common with **Zen Buddhism**, and in **the West**, with **Heraclitus** and **Derrida** (both discussed later).

NUMBERS

Pythagoras's almost mystical veneration for numbers laid the foundations for the modern scientific belief that maths is the key to understanding the universe.

 NAME PYTHAGORAS

 DATES C.570–C.495 BC

 NATIONALITY GREEK (SAMOS)

 SCHOOL PRE-SOCRATIC (PYTHAGOREAN)

 MAIN WORKS NO WRITINGS SURVIVE

 KEY CONTRIBUTIONS MATHS, METAPHYSICS

THE RATIONAL UNIVERSE

Pythagoras's name persists, of course, in the **mathematical theorem bearing his name** that relates to **right-angled triangles**.

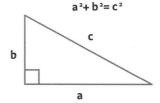

$$a^2 + b^2 = c^2$$

UNIVERSAL HARMONY

Pythagoras was so impressed with the **power and harmony of numbers, and their ability** to **describe reality**, that he **believed they formed** the **basis** of the **structure of the universe**, and that the **planets** themselves **emitted distinct musical tones**. Thus, the **spacing of the planets from the Earth** to the **final sphere** of the **fixed stars** corresponded to **musical intervals** (a theory that lives on in the phrase *the music of the spheres*).

THE IRRATIONAL

However, as one of Pythagoras's followers, **Hippasus of Metapontum** (c.530–c.450 BC), is said to have discovered, **not all numbers are rational** (that is, **expressible as the ratio of two whole numbers**). So, while 8 can be expressed as 8/1, or 16/2, etc., the **square root** of 8 ($\sqrt{8}$, or that number which, **multiplied by itself**, gives 8) cannot be expressed this way, but gives 2.82842712474619… a sequence that goes on and on, **never ending or repeating** – as, of course, does the most famous **irrational number**, *pi* (π), the **ratio of the circumference of a circle to its diameter**. Perhaps the universe is **not so rational after all**.

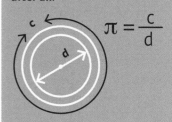

$$\pi = \frac{c}{d}$$

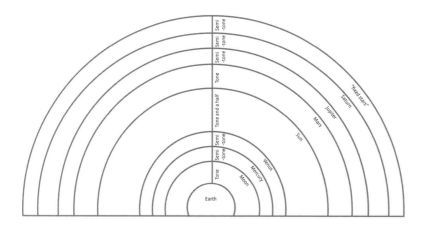

SUFFERING

Siddhartha Gautama taught that human desire led inevitably to suffering, the only solution to which was to practise a life of mindful and compassionate detachment.

 NAME SIDDHARTHA GAUTAMA (THE BUDDHA)

 DATES C.563–C.483 BC

 NATIONALITY INDIAN (NEPAL)

 SCHOOL BUDDHISM

 MAIN WORKS ORAL TEACHINGS LATER COLLECTED IN WRITTEN FORM

 KEY CONTRIBUTIONS ETHICS, METAPHYSICS, EPISTEMOLOGY

THE BUDDHA

Gautama – most commonly now known simply as **the Buddha** (**"enlightened one"**) – was thought to have been **a prince** in what is now **Nepal**, who **gave up his wealth** and **privilege** to become a **wandering monk** or **holy man**. After many years of exploring **different philosophies** and **traditions**, he **founded his own path**, which he termed the **Middle Way**.

DUKKHA

Buddha taught **Four Noble Truths**, the first of which is that **life is *dukkha*** (suffering). **All that lives, dies,** and we **cannot ultimately avoid the pain caused by disease and decay**. **Desire** is **never sated**, and **pleasure** and **beauty** are **short-lasting**, giving way to **yearning** and **loss**.

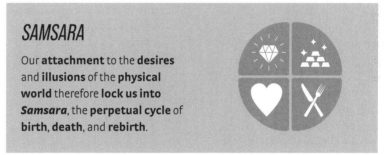

SAMSARA

Our **attachment** to the **desires** and **illusions** of the **physical world** therefore **lock us into** *Samsara*, the **perpetual cycle** of **birth**, **death**, and **rebirth**.

THE EIGHTFOLD PATH

To **escape this cycle** we must **practise the Middle Way** between the **extremes of ascetic self-denial** and **sensory overindulgence**, following the **Noble Eightfold Path**. This involved **renunciation** of **hedonistic** and **immoral practices**, **stilling** the **mind** and **emotions** through **meditation** in order to **detach from desire**, and thus **finally achieving insight** into the **true nature of existence**.

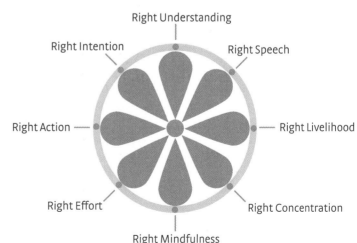

Right Understanding
Right Intention
Right Speech
Right Action
Right Livelihood
Right Effort
Right Concentration
Right Mindfulness

THE GOLDEN RULE

Confucius argued that the key to ensuring social order, political harmony, and personal moral integrity was the performance of defined social roles and respect for authority.

 NAME CONFUCIUS (KONGFUZI)

 DATES C.551 BC TO C.479 BC

 NATIONALITY CHINESE

 SCHOOL CONFUCIANISM

 MAIN WORKS *THE ANALECTS*

 KEY CONTRIBUTIONS ETHICS, POLITICAL PHILOSOPHY

THE SUPERIOR MAN

Kongfuzi (better known in the West as **Confucius**) was a **Chinese philosopher** who served variously as an **administrative official**, **teacher**, and **political advisor**. The central focus of his thought was the **correct behaviour** and **attitudes** of the "**superior man**", an **ideal ethical figure** whom we **should all seek to embody**. As such, Confucius was **less concerned with laying out specific ethical rules for particular situations** than with **cultivating virtuous qualities** that would **allow the individual to behave ethically in any context**.

REN

An important concept here is **Ren**, which may be variously translated as "**empathy**", "**love**", or "**benevolence**", but chiefly concerns our **right conduct with others**. Beginning with **those closest to us**, Confucius argued that **such an attitude should extend beyond our family and immediate friends** and out into the **community**, the **province**, and the **nation**. In **all our dealings**, we should **treat others as we ourselves would wish to be treated** – a precept that is **common to many moral and religious systems**, and has therefore become known as the **Golden Rule of ethics**.

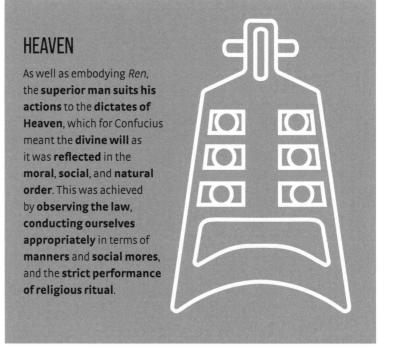

HEAVEN

As well as embodying *Ren*, the **superior man suits his actions** to the **dictates of Heaven**, which for Confucius meant the **divine will** as it was **reflected** in the **moral**, **social**, and **natural order**. This was achieved by **observing the law**, **conducting ourselves appropriately** in terms of **manners** and **social mores**, and the **strict performance of religious ritual**.

UNIVERSAL FLUX

Heraclitus was an obscure figure who questioned the human capacity to understand reality, which he considered to be in a constant state of flux.

 NAME HERACLITUS

DATES FL. C.500 BC

 NATIONALITY GREEK (EPHESUS)

 SCHOOL PRE-SOCRATIC

 MAIN WORKS ONLY FRAGMENTS SURVIVE

 KEY CONTRIBUTIONS EPISTEMOLOGY, METAPHYSICS

FIRE AND THE RIVER

Heraclitus is often grouped together with the **pre-Socratic natural philosophers**, where he is seen as **advancing a different candidate** for the **ultimate principle of reality**, comparing it to **fire**. He also **compared reality** to a **constantly flowing river**, a **state of perpetual change**, and where, **from moment to moment, nothing is the same**.

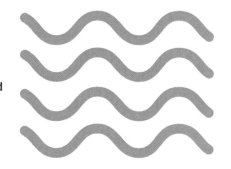

SCEPTICISM AND OBSCURITY

Obviously, this flux entails **problems for knowledge**, and Heraclitus was very **sceptical** of the **human capacity** to **achieve it**, seeming to hold a **low opinion of humanity in general**. He is reported to have written a **single book**, of which **only second-hand fragments survive**; it resembles more an **obscure poem** than a **philosophical text**, and (quite rightly) he thought most readers would not understand it. He also seems to have been generally **critical of philosophers**, arguing that **what often passed for knowledge** and **wisdom** was **superficial** and **suggested no true understanding**.

LOGOS

However, despite this somewhat **pessimistic view**, Heraclitus **does hold out some hope**. There is, he says, a **meaning to the world** that it is **possible for anyone to grasp** – what he termed its *logos* (**"word"**, **"message"**). The suggestion here is therefore perhaps **not that knowledge is impossible for human beings**, but that **most people – philosophers included** – are merely **going about it** in the **wrong way**.

PARADOX

Logical paradoxes have long been used to illustrate flaws in philosophical arguments, and Zeno used them to show that our common-sense understanding of time and space is wrong.

   NAME ZENO

DATES C.490–C.430 BC

NATIONALITY GREEK (ELEA)

   SCHOOL PRE-SOCRATIC (ELEATIC)

MAIN WORKS NO WRITINGS SURVIVE

KEY CONTRIBUTIONS METAPHYSICS

PARMENIDES

Zeno was a follower of the Greek philosopher **Parmenides** (c.515–c.440 BC), who argued for a position known as *monism*: that though the **world appears to consist of many different things**, it is **actually a unity**.

ACHILLES AND THE TORTOISE

Zeno's **most famous paradox** imagines **a race between the warrior Achilles and a tortoise**. Given a **head start**, the **tortoise can never be overtaken**, for **before he catches it, Achilles must get halfway**; and **before he closes the distance left**, he **must get halfway to *that* point**; and so on (a similar argument is made by Zeno's **paradox of the arrow** – replace tortoise with target, and Achilles with arrow). So, if we imagine the world to be **divided up** into **separate units of time and space**, Achilles will **never overtake the tortoise** (and the **arrow will never reach its target**).

DIVISIBILITY

Zeno also uses **paradox** to **argue against** the notion that the **world is made of many things** (such as **Democritus's atoms**, which we'll look at later). If, he says, we think of a **space** as made up of **multiple units** (e.g. inches), then each of those units can be divided to produce smaller units, and **so on to infinity**. However, this means that there can be **no ultimate indivisible units** out of which we can **build other things**, for **either such units will have no length to be divided**, or **everything is infinitely divisible**, just a **continuum without parts**.

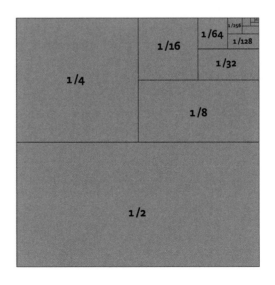

SOPHISM

Sophists were professional tutors whose skills in teaching logic and argument provided the foundation for the view that truth was simply a matter of having the best argument.

 NAME PROTAGORAS

 DATES C.490–C.420 BC

 NATIONALITY GREEK

 SCHOOL PRE-SOCRATIC (SOPHIST)

 MAIN WORKS ONLY FRAGMENTS SURVIVE

 KEY CONTRIBUTIONS EPISTEMOLOGY, ETHICS

IMMORAL TEACHINGS

Protagoras was one of the **earliest sophists**, and shares, with **Gorgias**, the dubious honour of being a **target of Plato's displeasure**. Plato's main concern was that, by **teaching skills in argument** and **reasoning** at the **expense of a genuine understanding of ethics**, sophists helped **foster immorality**.

CORRUPTERS OF YOUTH

Little of Protagoras's works has survived, and ironically we **know most about him** solely through the **dialogue of Plato** that bears his name – which is a bit like leaving your **reputation** in the hands of your **greatest critic**. So it's not surprising, perhaps, that the **modern view we have of sophists is as immoral mercenaries** – the *true* **corrupters** of the **young** (something of which **Plato's mentor Socrates** was **later falsely accused**).

RELATIVISM

Whether the sophists' **reputation** was **deserved or not** is **hard to say**. They certainly **accepted payment** – but what's wrong with that? The **worst** we can say about Protagoras himself, at least, seems to be that he was a *sceptic* and a *relativist*. He claimed that we **cannot know anything with certainty**, and that (Plato interprets him as saying) all our **concepts** and **values** are **relative**, **shaped** and **distorted** by our **necessarily human viewpoint** – that **"man is the measure of all things"**, as Protagoras himself put it. In this sense, however, **rather than a corrupter of youth**, Protagoras seems to be merely a **forerunner of certain strands of modern philosophy**, where such **scepticism** and **relativism do not now seem so radical**.

ATOMISM

The beginnings of the scientific notion that the universe consists of tiny particles of matter can ultimately be traced to the pre-Socratic Greek philosophers.

 NAME DEMOCRITUS

 DATES C.460–C.370 BC

 NATIONALITY GREEK

 SCHOOL PRE-SOCRATIC

 MAIN WORKS ONLY FRAGMENTS SURVIVE

 KEY CONTRIBUTIONS METAPHYSICS, ETHICS

EARLY ATOMISTS

While it is thought that the idea was first proposed by **Leucippus** (fl. fifth century BC), *atomism* is now **most often associated with his pupil, Democritus**. It was also later developed by **Epicurus** and the Roman philosopher **Lucretius** (c.94–c.55 BC). Like other **pre-Socratic philosophers**, Democritus was concerned with **the fundamental nature** of the **physical world**, but **rejected** the **idea** that the **ultimate constituent** was **air**, **fire**, **water**, or **some other perceptible element**.

INDIVISIBLE PARTICLES

Instead, Democritus argued that the **universe consisted of an infinite number of *atoms***. These are **tiny particles** that **could not be cut or divided** (*atom* means "**indivisible**"), being made of the **same material**, of **varying size** and **shape**, and **existing in a void**. The atoms' **different shapes** explained the **different properties and behaviour** of the **substances they formed**. A **solid substance**, such as **metal** or **stone**, might consist of atoms with **shapes that allowed close-fitting connections**, like **jigsaw pieces**, whereas **water** or **fire atoms** might possess a shape that enabled them to **move** or **flow over one another**.

atoms of water

atoms of stone

THE VOID

In all of this, the notion of the **void** was an important one, for **without the space to join and move apart**, there **could be no change, growth**, or **decay**. In fact, the way that **Nature** appeared to **disassemble** and **reassemble** things during such processes was perhaps itself **suggestive of the existence of these smaller "parts"**.

THE SOCRATIC METHOD

The Greek philosopher Socrates was deemed by the Delphic Oracle the wisest man in Athens, but what did that actually mean?

 NAME SOCRATES

 DATES C.469–399 BC

 NATIONALITY GREEK (ATHENS)

 SCHOOL CLASSICAL GREEK PHILOSOPHY

 MAIN WORKS NO WRITINGS SURVIVE

 KEY CONTRIBUTIONS ETHICS, EPISTEMOLOGY

SOCRATES

Socrates left behind **no written teachings**, preferring **discussion** and **debate**. His chief amusement seems to have involved **wandering around Athens annoying the populace** with his **constant questions**, and tormenting those who **claimed to know more than him**. For this reason, he thought of himself as a sort of **moral "gadfly"**. The motive behind all this seems to have been to **test the truth of the Oracle's pronouncement**.

SOCRATIC IGNORANCE

Since Socrates considered himself **anything but wise**, he reasoned that his wisdom must lie in the fact that he was the *only* **person who knew that he knew nothing**. This is, of course, a **cunning debating strategy**: it's more effective simply to allow your opponent to **tie themselves up in knots** in the **search for ultimate justifications**, for as any parent knows, there **must come a point where the "whys" stop**.

THE DELPHIC ORACLE

The **Pythia,** priestess of the **Temple of Apollo at Delphi**, was the most famous Oracle of the ancient world, consulted by the **famous and powerful** as well as **common folk**. Sat in a **perforated cauldron** placed on a tripod, she **inhaled fumes** that enabled her to enter a **trance**. The resulting **pronouncements** were often **enigmatic** and **ambiguous**.

SOCRATIC METHOD

"Socratic method" is still a much-favoured **educational technique**, allowing students to grasp a subject more securely by **reasoning their own way to the conclusion**. Socrates' pupil **Plato** would later use this method in an attempt to show that we **all possess some form of innate knowledge**, present from birth. In fact, since Socrates left **no written records** of his teachings, Plato's writings are the **only record we have of his mentor's beliefs**.

EUTHANASIA

Faced with execution or exile, Socrates chose to embody his belief that a "good death" was preferable to an unexamined life.

SOCRATES' CHOICE

As you might expect, revealing people's **ignorance** doesn't always go down well, and so it's perhaps no great surprise that Socrates found himself **hauled before the courts** on the **dubious charges of impiety** and **corrupting the youth**. Found **guilty**, and faced with the choice of **exile** or **death**, he chose the latter, reasoning that he would prefer to face whatever **judgement awaited him in the afterlife** than condone that imposed by **earthly judges**. In his own eyes, he'd done nothing wrong, and exile would banish him not only from the Athens that he loved, but also from the **life of enquiry** that he had pursued there. **Such an unexamined life**, he believed, **would not be worth living**.

A GOOD DEATH

Socrates' choice of a **"good death"** (the literal meaning of *euthanasia*) is an assertion that, faced with **extreme pain** or **mental suffering**, we might **legitimately choose to end our existence**. However, while some philosophers have condoned this view, others have opposed it, viewing **suicide** as **cowardly**, **immoral**, or even a sign of **mental illness**.

FORMS OF EUTHANASIA

Euthanasia comes in **three main forms**: **voluntary** (at the person's wishes), **involuntary** (**against** the person's wishes), and **non-voluntary** (where the person is **incapable of expressing a preference**). Each of these may be achieved by different means: **active** (e.g. **drug overdose**) or **passive** (e.g. **withholding treatment**).

DEATH BY HEMLOCK

Socrates chose to **take his own life** by drinking a **tea** made from the poison **hemlock**, a drug that was commonly used in **Classical times** to **execute prisoners**, and that caused gradual **loss of sensation and paralysis**, eventually resulting in **respiratory failure**.

UNIVERSALS

Plato argued that all knowledge depends on independently existing universal ideas or Forms, a doctrine that he illustrated through his famous allegory of the Cave.

 NAME PLATO

 DATES C.428–C.347 BC

 NATIONALITY GREEK (ATHENS)

 SCHOOL CLASSICAL GREEK PHILOSOPHY

 MAIN WORKS *APOLOGY; REPUBLIC; GORGIAS; SYMPOSIUM; MENO*

 KEY CONTRIBUTIONS ETHICS, EPISTEMOLOGY, METAPHYSICS, AESTHETICS, POLITICAL PHILOSOPHY

IGNORANCE

You are **tied up** in a **dark cave**. Against the wall, you barely discern strange **moving shadows**. You are then **released**, and turn around to see that the shadows are cast by **statues passing before a fire**. You **exit the cave** and pass into the **outside world**, to look up at the **Sun**.

THE FORMS

Because the **senses will always mislead us**, only **rational ideas** can help us **truly understand** the world. For example, take the statement "**Dogs** have **four legs**." **Cats** have four legs, too, as do **horses**. What makes a dog a dog, not a cat or a horse, and means that spaniels, terriers, Rottweilers, etc., all have something in common? It is the **universal idea** or *Form* of the dog, **without which we could not make sense of the statement** – or the world.

THE TWO WORLDS

Plato's peculiar **allegory** – which I've simplified here – is meant to illustrate the **journey of the philosopher**. The **two worlds** – inside and outside the cave – represent the **visible and intelligible worlds respectively**. The **shadows** in the cave represent **physical appearances**, the **deceitful illusions** presented to us by the **senses**. Gradually, we begin to **make sense of these** (the **objects before the fire**), but it is **only when we enter the world of pure thought** (**leave the cave**) and undertake **rational analysis of ideas** (view the **objects outside** in the **daylight**), that we achieve **true knowledge** and **certainty**, through the **light of truth** and **goodness** (the **Sun**).

"All dogs echo the perfect *idea* of a dog"

MORAL REALISM

As our knowledge of the physical world requires the independent existence of universal ideas, so for Plato did our moral actions require a universal standard of goodness.

THE DIALOGUES

Most of **Plato's work** is presented in the form of **dramatic dialogue**, usually involving a **fictionalized Socrates** as he **interrogates opponents** on various topics. A number of these centre around **ethics**, where Socrates debates with those who argue that (for instance) **morality** is merely a **matter of convention**, or that **"might is right"**. In contrast, Socrates – as Plato's mouthpiece, perhaps – argues that **moral goodness** is a **real, independent quality distinct from self-interest and social convention**, and **being good** is in fact **more akin to being healthy**.

THE RING OF GYGES

To illustrate this, in the **Republic** Plato invokes the **Ring of Gyges**, a **mythical object** that was said to make the **wearer invisible**, and therefore **free to perform any act without fear of capture or punishment**. Would someone who wore such a ring be "**happy**"? Plato says not, because **being happy requires being good**, and our own **bad actions** actually **cause us harm**.

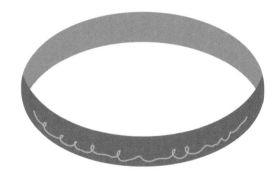

TRUE HARM

In the **Gorgias**, **Socrates** argues that it is **impossible for a good man to suffer harm**, because true "harm" involves **harm to the soul** (creating **moral bad habits** and **mental imbalance**), in comparison with which **physical suffering**, even **torture**, is nothing. In contrast, the **apparently enviable man** – Gyges, or the **all-powerful tyrant** who can **fulfil any desire** – is viewed rather as someone so **at the whim of his own passions** that he is in fact **enslaved by them**.

THE IDEAL STATE

The structure of Plato's perfect society reflected the moral and physical health of the ideal individual, and what fostered goodness in the person produced justice in the state.

THE TRIPARTITE SOUL

Plato divided the **soul** into **three aspects**: **mind**, **spirit** (**emotion**), and **appetite**. Ideally, the **rational mind** directed the **emotions** to keep **desire** in check. However, if the mind was **not developed enough**, or the individual **valued emotions or desire above reason**, the person could develop **unhealthy and immoral habits**.

THE GUARDIANS

As **mind** should **rule the body**, so – Plato reasoned – those with the **best-developed mental faculties** should rule the state (thus making it a form of **aristocracy** – literally, "**rulership by the best**"). Accordingly, he envisaged an **educational programme** where the **most promising children** were hot-housed, given **special physical and mental training**, and set aside to be **Guardians** – the **stock** from which **rulers** (Guardians proper) and **auxiliaries** (lesser talented Guardians, who become soldiers and ministers) would be drawn. The rest of the society – the **common folk** – would be concerned mostly with **producing goods – farming**, **fishing**, **weaving** and **smithing**, and so on.

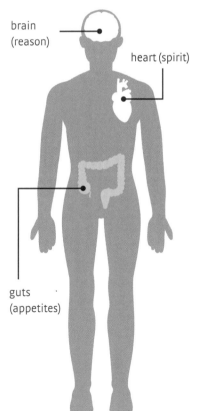

brain
(reason)

heart (spirit)

guts
(appetites)

UNJUST STATES

Just as the **ideal individual** reflected the **perfect state** (**utopia**), so **imbalanced or immoral individuals** reflected the **ways in which states could go wrong** (**unjust states**). Of these, in order of **progressive deterioration** from his ideal society, Plato listed **four other forms of government**: **timocracy** (rulership by the **warrior class**), **oligarchy** (rulership by the **rich**), **democracy** (rulership by the **people**), and **tyranny** (rulership by a **single individual**). Of these, it's notable that **democracy is next to worst**, because it effectively represents rulership by the **bodily desires** (which, in Plato's scheme, is what the **populace** represents).

TIMOCRACY

OLIGARCHY

DEMOCRACY

TYRANNY

ART AND LIES

Notoriously, Plato banished poetry from his ideal state, arguing that it peddled untruths and appealed mostly to the emotions.

THE PERFECT BED

For **Plato**, all forms of **art** were a distant cousin of **truth**. What did he mean by this? If you recall his **allegory of the Cave**, there were various **steps from ignorance to knowledge**; from the **shadows** on the wall (**sense impressions**) to the things **outside the cave** (the **true ideas**). Plato uses the example of a **bed**: a **physical bed** is **not the true thing**, but merely a **copy** of the **perfect idea** or *Form* of a bed. And what therefore is a poem about a bed? A copy of a copy. **Poets** and **painters**, therefore, are even **further from truth than craftsmen**.

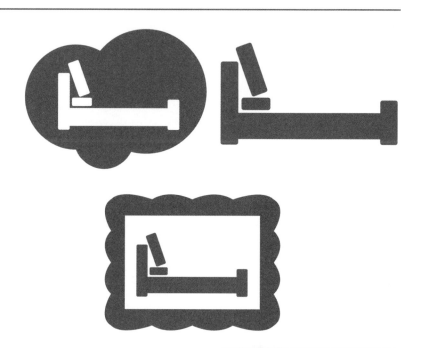

PROPAGANDA

But Plato's **ideal republic** is **not devoid of art**, and he is especially fond of **music**, writing of the various ways it can be employed to **train and discipline people**. The point, then, is **not that poetry in itself is bad**, but that **bad poets are bad for the state**. If artists and poets could be guided to produce the *right types* of art (*propaganda* that served **political purposes**), they would presumably be welcome. However, what Plato has effectively invented here is **censorship**: the idea that **only certain forms of creativity** are **allowed**.

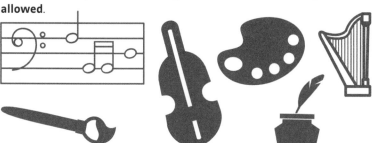

THE GOLDEN LIE

It is ironic, perhaps, that having railed against poetry for its **lack of truthfulness**, Plato finds himself employing his own **subtly crafted lie** in **service of the state**. Admitting that people are **not really born into neat types** (rulers, soldiers, producers), he argues nonetheless that the **health of the state** requires people to **believe that**. He therefore invents a **"golden lie"** to **justify this social division**. Lies in the **service of truth** are fine, it seems.

26

CYNICISM

In living a life of bare necessity, Diogenes attempted to highlight the shallowness and moral hypocrisy of his contemporary citizens, whom he believed had lost touch with the fundamental truths of human existence.

 NAME DIOGENES OF SINOPE

 DATES C.412 BC–323 BC

 NATIONALITY GREEK

 SCHOOL CYNICISM

 MAIN WORKS NONE SURVIVE

 KEY CONTRIBUTIONS ETHICS, EPISTEMOLOGY, METAPHYSICS, AESTHETICS, POLITICAL PHILOSOPHY

ALEXANDER THE GREAT

None of Diogenes's writings survive, but he is most celebrated for his **practical example** of **simplicity**, **integrity**, and **fearless honesty**. He is said to have **lived on the streets** with **only a large barrel for shelter**, **subsisting on charity** and with **meagre possessions**, freely **passing judgement** on all who passed. For instance, one story relates how he was asked by **Alexander the Great** whether there was anything the **great ruler could do for Diogenes**, only to be told that, actually, he was **blocking the nice warm sunlight**, so it would be **nice if he moved aside**.

THE FACTS OF LIFE

Though this story is **apocryphal**, it **perfectly captures one key element of Diogenes's teachings**: **social status doesn't matter**. Whether you are a **king** or a **slave**, a **celebrated warrior** or a **beggar**, you are **still a human being**, and as such someone who must **eat**, **drink**, **feel sexual urges**, **go to the toilet**, and eventually **get old** and **die**. Why then are we so **ashamed of our humanity**? Why do we try to **disguise it** with **false airs and graces**, and **create artificial distinctions** between our fellow beings?

DOGS

Diogenes was a key figure in the movement that has become known as **Cynicism**, from the Greek **kynikos**, meaning "dog-like". This stems from the practitioners' **admiration** for the **animal's honest, natural, uncomplicated life**, which cynics **emulated** and considered a **good example for a society that had lost touch with these qualities**, and whose **shallow existence** these philosophers **"cynically" questioned** and **exposed**.

VIRTUE

Aristotle rejected Plato's notion of ethical conduct as based purely on intellectual knowledge of the Good, preferring to see it as the successful development of character.

 NAME ARISTOTLE

 DATES 384–322 BC

 NATIONALITY GREEK (ATHENS)

 SCHOOL CLASSICAL GREEK PHILOSOPHY

 MAIN WORKS *ETHICS; POLITICS; PHYSICS; ON THE SOUL; POETICS*

 KEY CONTRIBUTIONS ETHICS, POLITICAL PHILOSOPHY, AESTHETICS, METAPHYSICS, LOGIC, PHILOSOPHY OF MIND

MORAL IGNORANCE

Plato considered that people did **not do wrong deliberately**, but only through **ignorance. Corrected of their misunderstanding**, they would thereafter **choose the right path**. However, **Aristotle** thought **wrongdoing** was **more complicated** than this, and that **acting morally involved more** than **mere intellectual education**.

THE GOLDEN MEAN

Doing the right thing requires **experience**, he argued. Many **qualities** can be expressed in **one of two extremes. Too much** or **too little** can produce **bad results**, but the **right action** – the *golden mean*, as it's been termed – is **often a middle point**. A **brave man** is neither **rash** nor **cowardly**, but somewhere **in between**; the right attitude to **money** is to neither **hoard it** nor to **blow it all**; the right attitude to **food** is neither to **gorge** nor to **starve**.

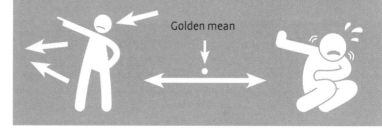

Golden mean

TARGET PRACTICE

But things are **not quite so simple**. We need to learn just **how to apply these qualities** in the **right way** given the **circumstances**. As such, the **development of virtue** is **not an exact science**, but requires **time** and **experience** to hit the right mark. This approach is known as *virtue ethics*.

AKRASIA

But to **develop one's character** one also needed to **train oneself** to **keep the passions and desires in check**. As such, while **some wrongdoing** was in fact **due to lack of knowledge** (as Plato argued), **some** was **also due** to *akrasia*, or **weakness of the will**. We **know what the right thing is**, but – because we have **not acquired sufficient discipline** – are **unable to do it**.

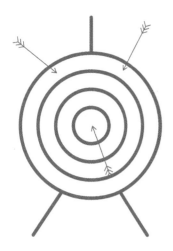

TELEOLOGY

Aristotle argued that everything that exists has some purpose or role it must fulfil, and that – he implied – was a direct consequence of its being created.

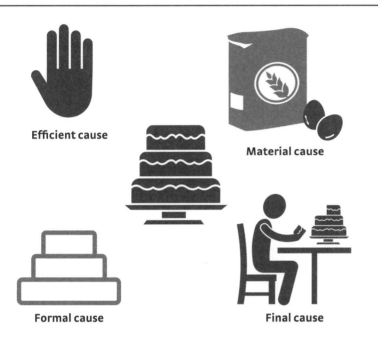

Efficient cause

Material cause

Formal cause

Final cause

FOUR CAUSES

In the **Aristotelian system**, every individual item could be **understood** in terms of **four "causes"**. That which **caused it to exist** was its *efficient cause*. The material it was **made from** was its *material cause*. The **shape it took** was its *formal cause*. And its **role** or **purpose for existing** was its *final cause*. If we take a **cake**, then its **efficient cause** is the **baker**, its **material cause** is its **various ingredients**, its **formal cause** is its **overall shape** and **design**, and its **final cause** would be for **people to eat**.

PURPOSE

In **modern times**, we don't now think of a thing's **matter** or **form** as **"causes"**; we **reserve that term** for the **efficient cause** (that which **causes something to exist in its current form**). The notion of a **final form** has mostly **fallen out of use** – scientifically, at least – because it **implies a designer or creator** that has some idea of a thing's intended purpose. This is simple if the object is **manmade** – a cake or a chair – but what if it's a **natural object**? What is the **purpose** of a **tree** or a **stone**? And **who would give it that purpose**? The answer, for **Aristotle**, was **God**.

THE DESIGN ARGUMENT

The idea that the **natural** and **physical world** shows **evidence of design** is of course a well-known **argument for the existence of God**. Also called the *teleological argument* (from the Greek *telos*, meaning **"purpose"**), it argues that there must be a *final cause* to **everything that exists** (to use **Aristotle's phrase**). As we'll see later, however, this remains a **controversial** topic.

CITIZENSHIP

Just as friendship played a key role in ethical development, Aristotle saw citizenship as essential to helping human beings flourish.

POLITICAL NATURALISM

Aristotle's political views follow directly from his **ethics**. If the **purpose of human life** is to **fulfil human potential**, then the **ideal form of government** will help **realize that**. And since, he argued, we are **by nature** "**political animals**" (a view known as ***political naturalism***), such potential can **only be fulfilled** through a **communal life of political engagement**.

FORMS OF GOVERNMENT

Aristotle identified **six possible types of political organization**, differing according to the **number of rulers** and **in whose interest they ruled**. A **single individual** might be a **hedonistic tyrant** or an **honourable monarch**, depending on whether they **served self-interest** or the **common good**. Similarly, a **small elite** could be a **greedy oligarchy** or a **virtuous aristocracy**. And lastly, **rulership by the people** might result in a **licentious majority-serving democracy** (like **Plato**, Aristotle was **not a fan**), or a **stable polity**, guided by **group wisdom**.

Aristotle's Classification		
Number of Rulers	**Serving Common Good**	**Serving Self-Interest**
Single monarch	👑 Monarchy	Tyranny
Elite few	Aristocracy	Oligarchy
Democratic majority	🤝 Polity	Democracy

THE MIXED CONSTITUTION

Since **virtuous elites** and **wise monarchs** are **rare**, a **polity** was both the **least worst** and **most likely** option, where a **strong "middle class"** – **neither rich nor poor** – **combined the virtues** and **avoided the faults** of the **other forms of governance**. Such a **mixed society** would ensure that **no one** was **excluded** or **dominated** (thereby **minimizing risk of revolt**), and **encourage citizens** to play a **full role in civic life**.

WOMEN AND SLAVES

Aristotle has in mind here the sort of **city-state** (***polis***) prevalent in **Greece** at the time, the **small size** of which allowed citizens to **participate directly** in **councils, juries**, and **assemblies**. But such **public engagement** could **only be achieved** through **slavery** and the **subjugation of women**, whose **servitude** provided **selected citizens** with the **quality of life** and **leisure** necessary for the **contemplation** and **political engagement** Aristotle envisaged.

CATHARIS

Aristotle proposed that the purpose of great art was to educate us about human nature, and in the process to provide both emotional release and intellectual insight.

TRAGIC DRAMA

Why do we like to watch terrifying **horror films** or read **sad stories**? Is it out of some **sadistic enjoyment of another's misfortune**, or a **masochistic pleasure at our own sympathetic pain**? Aristotle argued that such depictions – in his times, the **tragic drama** of **Euripides' *Medea***, for instance, or **Sophocles' *Oedipus Rex*** – actually served the purpose of ***katharsis***, which involved **purging the audience of negative emotions**, especially those of **fear** and **pity**.

IMITATION

But this is not the **only purpose of tragic art**, and Aristotle spends much of his ***Poetics*** outlining how a **key function of dramatization** also involves ***mimesis***, which is the **process of imitating** and **representing life** in **artistic form**. By seeing **people** and **events objectified** and **personified**, we are in a **better position to understand them**.

PSYCHOLOGICAL INSIGHT

But this process of **objectification** also perhaps gives us a clue as to **another function of catharsis**, whereby we are better able to **distance ourselves** from **normally distressing events** in order to gain **greater insight into them** – **what led to them**, the **character flaws that bred them**, and therefore perhaps **how we might avoid a similar fate**. Some **modern interpreters of Aristotle** therefore argue that **catharsis** is better understood as **a process whereby we achieve a form of intellectual insight**. A **modern playgoer** can feel both **distressed** and **enlightened** at Shakespeare's **skilful depiction** of **Othello's slow descent into irrational jealousy**, feeling at once **greater compassion for his misdeeds** while coming to a **deeper understanding** of how the **seed of his tragic flaw** is **present in us all**.

FRIENDSHIP

For Aristotle, choosing the right friends in life was not just key to happiness, but essential to living a truly moral life.

PHILIA

Aristotle has in mind here not our narrower **modern definition of friendship**, but a **broader concept of social relationship** (*philia*). This includes **family**, **close friends**, **neighbours**, but also **work colleagues**, the man who works in the **corner shop**, or your son's **teacher** – basically, **anyone with whom we might be on friendly terms**.

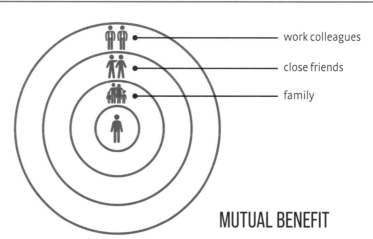

- work colleagues
- close friends
- family

MUTUAL BENEFIT

Aristotle argued that **true friendship is mutual**. You **wish the best for one another**. But **what is "the best"? Jim shares your interest in cars**, but you are, in a sense, **taking advantage of one another to make money**. You might **enjoy drinking in Tina's company**, but you **never see her otherwise**, and she's **mainly interested in a good time** and **blowing off steam**. Therefore, in **providing a space to talk about your personal lives**, your **aspirations**, your **troubles** and **worries**, it is **only Steve's friendship** that seems to be **based on something deeper**. **True friendship**, Aristotle argued, is **not just about mutual advantage**, or **mutual pleasure**, but about **helping each other to be better, happier people**, and in so doing come closer to **realizing our potential and living a worthwhile life**.

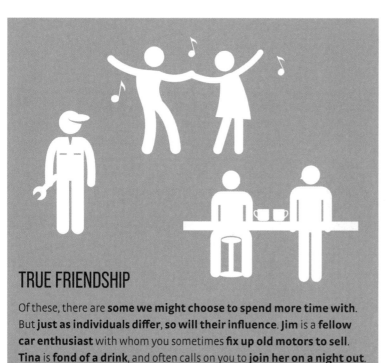

TRUE FRIENDSHIP

Of these, there are **some we might choose to spend more time with**. But **just as individuals differ, so will their influence. Jim** is a **fellow car enthusiast** with whom you sometimes **fix up old motors to sell**. **Tina** is **fond of a drink**, and often calls on you to **join her on a night out**. **Steve** is someone you like to **meet for a chat over coffee**, where you **discuss what's happening in each other's lives**. But **which, if any, are** *true* **friends?**

ILLUSION

The scepticism of Chinese Daoist philosopher Zhuangzi reflects a concern that has dogged philosophers of all ages and traditions: how do we know what is real?

 NAME ZHUANGZI

 DATES FL. C. FOURTH CENTURY BC

 NATIONALITY CHINESE

 SCHOOL DAOISM

 MAIN WORKS *THE ZHUANGZI*

 KEY CONTRIBUTIONS EPISTEMOLOGY

THE BUTTERFLY

What **little we know of Zhuangzi** – a follower of **Laozi** – comes mostly from the **text that bears his name**, itself a **later collection of stories and sayings purportedly originating from the philosopher himself**. Of these, the most famous tells how, one night, Zhuangzi **dreams that he is a butterfly**, but **when the dream ends** he realizes that he is **uncertain whether he is now Zhuangzi**, having **merely dreamt that he is a butterfly**, or a **butterfly**, now **dreaming that he is Zhuangzi**.

ZEN

The ***Zhuangzi*** is full of such **challenges to our common-sense view of reality**, and its **anti-intellectual approach to knowledge** was to be an **influence upon later Zen Buddhism** (explored more fully later). Perhaps, seen in this light, the **riddle is not meant to have a neat solution**, but is instead an attempt to **paralyze our thoughts** with an **insoluble paradox** in order to **release our minds from pointless intellectualizing**, **free** at last to **appreciate true reality**.

VEIL OF PERCEPTION

However, the **Western philosophical tradition** has **largely taken a different route**, attempting to establish a **rational guarantee that we know what is real**, that we can **trust our senses**, and that we can **tell whether we are dreaming or not** (a challenge taken up by **Descartes**, whom we discuss later). The problem with this endeavour, of course, is that **almost all our knowledge comes through the senses**. As such, some philosophers argue, our **perception of reality can never be direct**, but must necessarily be **filtered** through a ***veil of perception*** that we **cannot see or reason beyond**.

MODERATION

Epicurus is most known for promoting pleasure as the chief good, but his true doctrine favoured a form of ethical moderation.

 NAME EPICURUS

 DATES 341–270 BC

 NATIONALITY GREEK (SAMOS)

 SCHOOL EPICUREAN

 MAIN WORKS ONLY FRAGMENTS AND SHORT WRITINGS SURVIVE

 KEY CONTRIBUTIONS ETHICS, EPISTEMOLOGY, PHILOSOPHY OF RELIGION

PLEASURE

A **modern *epicurean*** is someone who **enjoys fine food and drink**, and **Epicurus's reputation** through the Middle Ages and into most of modern times was of someone who preached **sensual gratification**. But Epicurus's **true notion of good** was **not the excess** of the **hedonist**, nor even the **cultivated enjoyment** of the ***gourmand*** or aesthete, but the **simple pleasures** of the **humble life**.

ETHICS

In terms of **how we should live our lives**, Epicurus seems to have been **largely conformist** in his principles, arguing that the **guilt** we incur from **acting badly towards others** is the **strongest disincentive to bad behaviour**. **Acting morally**, he believed, leaves us with an **untroubled conscience** and the **tranquillity of mind** that he considered the **essence of happiness**.

FEAR AND PAIN

Epicurus therefore **divided the pleasures** into **those that could be pursued without any attendant anxiety or suffering**, and **those that could not**. **Rich food** gives us **indigestion**, **sexual love** can lead to **jealousy** and **heartbreak**, but the **gentler pastimes** of such things as the **conversation of friends** and the **pursuit of philosophical knowledge** were **beneficial without causing suffering**. In **all actions**, he argued, the **main goal** was **tranquillity of mind**.

DEATH

Regarding the emotions that disturb the mind, Epicurus considered the chief of these to be anxiety concerning one's own death.

THE AFTERLIFE

While **not an atheist**, **Epicurus** considered that the **gods** were **far different from those depicted in Greek mythology**, and existed in a state **a long way removed from human affairs**. Perhaps for these reasons, he considered that they were **not concerned with the moral misdemeanours of human beings**, and there was therefore **no afterlife court of judgement** in which our **souls might be weighed** before being dispatched to a fate of **fitting reward or torment**.

NON-EXISTENCE

However, his chief reason for **not fearing death** seems to be have been that **the dead simply do not exist**. And since we **cannot fear that which we will not live to experience**, what is there to be afraid of? When death comes, you will **no longer be alive** (or **conscious** or **sensible**). So until then, **enjoy your life**. Death, then, is **not a state to be** *feared*, but simply a **cessation of all states, fear included**.

FACING DEATH

But what of the **anxiety** you feel due to your ***approaching*** death? What of the **sorrow** you feel for the impending **separation from your loved ones**, or the **things you will leave undone**? Or what if your death should be **painful**? Aren't these things **worth worrying about**? As if to settle these questions, rather like **Socrates**, Epicurus seems to have **approached his death** in a **remarkably cheerful manner**. Dying in **extreme pain**, he nonetheless **taught** and **chatted** happily right up **until the end**.

POSTHUMOUS HARM

In contrast, **Thomas Nagel** (b.1937) has argued that **death is in fact a bad thing**, robbing us of something of **positive value** (life). **Joel Feinberg** (1926–2004) also argues that, even if there is **no afterlife**, to slander the deceased's reputation harms their **"posthumous interests"** (those projects and influences they hoped would continue after their death).

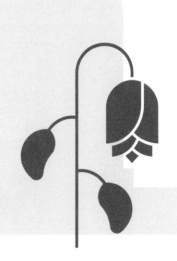

THE PROBLEM OF EVIL

If God is both able and willing to prevent the unnecessary suffering of innocent people, then why – asked Epicurus – does it continue? Why does evil exist?

Natural

TYPES OF EVIL

Theological discussion often divides **evil** into **two main types**: **moral** and **natural**. **Moral evil** involves the **conscious acts** of individuals, such as **murder** or **torture**, while **natural evil** involves "**acts of God**", such as **earthquakes**, **floods**, **famines** – assuming, of course, that these are **not manmade** (e.g. a consequence of **climate change**).

Moral

PURPOSE

As **traditionally conceived**, the **God of monotheism** is **omnipotent** (**all-powerful**) and **omni-benevolent** (**absolutely good**). These two qualities alone would seem enough to **question the existence of evil**, for surely they mean that he is **both able and willing to prevent moral injustice and natural disasters**. And, of course, if we add the commonly attributed quality of **omniscience** (being **all-knowing**), we can also ask: **if God** cannot but be **aware of human suffering**, and **would** and **could intervene**, **why** in fact **doesn't he**? Together, these three qualities produce what has been called the **Inconsistent Triad**.

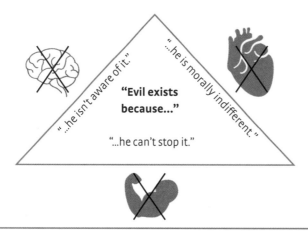

"...he isn't aware of it."

"...he is morally indifferent."

"Evil exists because..."

"...he can't stop it."

THEODICIES

As we've seen, **Epicurus** believed that the **gods** were **distant from human affairs**, and this might in turn provide an **explanation** of **how evil exists despite divine capabilities**: God (or the gods) is **simply not aware**. Such an explanation is termed a **theodicy**, and there have been numerous theodicies advanced through history, each proposing a different solution – perhaps evil **serves a purpose**, for instance, or God is **not allowed to interfere** with **human free will**. We'll look at some of these later, but the **central issue** is what **justification** or **rationale** could **explain** the **apparently purposeless suffering** of the **innocent** and the **powerless**.

JUST WAR

Just War Theory explores the conditions under which a state may be seen as justified in going to war, and what means it may legitimately employ.

 NAME MARCUS TULLIUS CICERO

 DATES 106–43 BC

 NATIONALITY ROMAN

 SCHOOL ECLECTICISM

 MAIN WORKS *ON DUTIES; ON THE NATURE OF THE GODS; ON THE ORATO*

 KEY CONTRIBUTIONS POLITICAL PHILOSOPHY

ON DUTIES

Some version of **Just War Theory** is **common** to many **cultures** and **traditions**. In the West, the question was briefly raised by both **Plato** and **Aristotle**, but a fuller account was later provided by Roman philosopher and statesman **Cicero**. In his **De Officiis** ("**On Duties**") he argued that war not only requires **sound motives**, but must be conducted in the **right manner**. Subsequent debate has **mostly followed Cicero's distinction**, and these two sets of criteria are now generally known by the medieval Latin terms *jus ad bellum* (**just cause for war**) and *jus in bello* (**right conduct in war**)

JUS AD BELLUM

A just war should really be an **act of self-defence**, **retaliation** for **unwarranted aggression**, and be a **last resort**. It should be waged by a **legitimate authority** (e.g. an **elected government**), and the response should be **proportionate** (an **eye for an eye** – but **no more**).

JUS IN BELLO

But war should also be conducted **appropriately**. We **shouldn't mistreat prisoners of war**, **target civilians**, nor aim at the **wilful destruction** of **non-strategic targets** and **property**.

MODERN WARFARE

In modern times, while such treaties as the **Geneva Conventions** have attempted to **shore up these principles**, we can see that **many conflicts flout them**. **Civilians** are now often considered "**collateral damage**", and the notion of "**pre-emptive war**" – often associated with **President G. W. Bush's "War on Terror"** – assumes that even a **perceived** or **potential future threat** may constitute **sufficient justification** for **military aggression** or **invasion**.

STOICISM

The Stoics taught that human destiny was in the hands of God or fate, but that happiness could be achieved by training the mind to live in harmony with Nature.

 NAME LUCIUS ANNAEUS SENECA

 DATES 4 BC–65 AD

 NATIONALITY ROMAN

 SCHOOL STOICISM

 MAIN WORKS *MORAL LETTERS TO LUCILIUS*

 KEY CONTRIBUTIONS ETHICS

ZENO'S PORCH

In the modern sense a "**stoical**" person is someone who remains **steadfast** in the face of **hardship** or **adversity**. But the term originates from the **Greek word *stoa***, meaning "**porch**", from the place where the **founder of Stoicism, Zeno of Citium** (c.333–c.263 BC), was wont to **teach**. (By the way, this was a **different Zeno** to the **lover of paradoxes, Zeno of Elea**, discussed earlier.)

NATURE

The Stoic tradition draws on **Cynicism, Epicureanism** and the teachings of **Aristotle**, and was hugely **influential** in the **Classical world**, especially at the height of the **Roman Empire**, counting among its **adherents** both **slaves** (**Epictetus**, 55–135 AD) and **emperors** (**Marcus Aurelius**, 121–80 AD). Stoics believed that the **whole of Nature** (a term that included all **organic** and **inorganic life**) is a **single unified organism**, whose function is **ordered by a god-like mind**. As parts of this organism, **humans do not possess free will**, but **happiness** is **still possible** by cultivating **emotional detachment** and a **wise acceptance** of the role determined by **fate**.

SENECA

One of the most celebrated Stoics was **Seneca the Younger**, as he is generally known (to **differentiate him from his father**, a writer of the same name). As a **statesman** and **tragic playwright**, Seneca's Stoicism informed both his **writings** and his **life**, and his **suicide**, ordered by the despotic Emperor Nero – the philosopher lay in his bath, calmly setting his affairs in order while Nero's soldiers stood by – became a **celebrated example** of the **typical Stoic virtues** of **equanimity** and **courage** in the **face of death**.

THE IRENAEAN THEODICY

The Greek bishop Irenaeus argued that evil exists because it is necessary to God's plan for the full development of the human soul.

 NAME ST IRENAEUS

 DATES C.130–C.202

 NATIONALITY GREEK

 SCHOOL CHRISTIAN

 MAIN WORKS *AGAINST HERESIES*

 KEY CONTRIBUTIONS PHILOSOPHY OF RELIGION

SPIRITUAL DEVELOPMENT

Irenaeus did not deny that **God created evil**, but argued that the **reason for its existence** was that **only through facing challenges** and **suffering** could the **human soul evolve** to its **full potential**. As such, **evil** may be seen as a sort of **training ground for spiritual development**.

GOD'S LIKENESS

The reason for this **need for development**, Irenaeus argued, was that **humans** are **created** only **in God's image** and **not in his** *likeness*. In order to **evolve from one to the other**, they must make certain **free will choices**. Built into this *theodicy* is therefore an **element** of the **free will defence** (later employed by **Augustine**, which we'll look at shortly).

epistemic distance

NEEDLESS SUFFERING

The **problem** with this form of theodicy, however, is that it would seem to **allow for the existence** of **needless suffering**. If an **infant** or a **young child suffers** and **dies**, what **opportunity** has there been for them to **develop**? Developing his **own form of Irenaean theodicy**, English philosopher **John Hick** (1922–2012) argued that such **apparently needless suffering** serves the purpose of **allowing others** to **feel pity** and **compassion**. If all **suffering** seemed **justified**, then it **would not allow us to develop these emotional qualities**. Hick also highlighted how this approach involves the idea that human beings must develop in *epistemic distance* from God: that is, **divorced from intellectual knowledge of God's existence**, so that **faith** must be a **freely chosen act**.

ORIGINAL SIN

St Augustine argued that all humans inherited the nature of Adam, and that the existence of evil was therefore a consequence of the corruption of human free will.

 NAME ST AUGUSTINE OF HIPPO

 DATES 354–430

 NATIONALITY ROMAN (ALGERIAN)

 SCHOOL CHRISTIAN

 MAIN WORKS *CONFESSIONS; CITY OF GOD*

 KEY CONTRIBUTIONS PHILOSOPHY OF RELIGION, ETHICS

CONCUPISCENCE

However, in certain **Judaeo-Christian traditions**, the doctrine of **original sin** proposes that **humanity** is **collectively tainted** by the **disobedience of Adam and Eve** in **eating from the Tree of Knowledge** in the **Garden of Eden**. St **Augustine** developed this **doctrine** further, arguing that **not only do we inherit Adam and Eve's guilt**, but that, since we are descended from them, our **bodily instincts** are **corrupted** by that **first act of disobedience**. As a result, certain forms of **desire** (what he termed *concupiscence*) are **necessarily sinful**, and it is only by **God's grace** that we can be redeemed from their influence.

COLLECTIVE GUILT

The notion of **divine punishment** for **disobedience** is **common** to many **religions** and **mythologies**. In **Greek mythology**, the titan **Prometheus** was punished by having his **liver pecked out** by an eagle **every day for eternity**, only for it to **regrow at night**. In **Norse mythology**, the **trickster god Loki** is **bound to a rock** over which a **venomous snake perpetually drips poison**.

THEODICY

Out of this doctrine, Augustine also developed a *theodicy* or **explanation** for the **existence of evil**. Unlike **Irenaeus**, Augustine argued that since God was **all-good**, he **could not have created evil**; rather, it was a **negative quality** – an **absence of God**. In **disobeying** and **turning away** from God, Adam therefore **corrupted his own will with evil**, and for us, as **Adam's descendants**, the **presence of evil** in the world is therefore both a **consequence** of and a **punishment** for this **first act of rebellion**.

NEOPLATONISM

Originating in third-century Egypt, Neoplatonism blended contemporary religion and philosophy with a mystical interpretation of Plato's doctrines.

 NAME PLOTINUS

 DATES C. 204–70 AD

 NATIONALITY EGYPTIAN

 SCHOOL CHRISTIAN

 MAIN WORKS *THE ENNEADS*

 KEY CONTRIBUTIONS METAPHYSICS

THE ONE

Neoplatonism is generally considered to have begun with **Plotinus**, an Egyptian philosopher in what was then part of the Roman Empire. Plotinus emphasizes **Plato's distrust of the physical world**, advancing a form of **monism**, which saw the **ultimate reality – the One –** as a **simple** and **indivisible God-like entity** that is at once the **origin** of **goodness**, **beauty**, and **truth**, and from which **all existing things *emanate***, while itself **remaining beyond them (*transcendent*)**.

UNION

Whereas **Aristotle** had defined **happiness** in terms that in part depended on **material** and **social** factors, **Plotinus** argued that true happiness is **independent of all such things**. Since the One is the **source of all things**, then by **unifying with it** through **meditation** and **intellectual contemplation** (*henosis*) we may achieve a **state of being** that is **immune** to the **buffetings of circumstance**.

INFLUENCE

While there is some debate as to what degree it reflects **genuine Platonism** – one tradition is that it **expounds Plato's lost writings or "hidden" doctrines** – the **impact of Neoplatonism** has been **vast**. It was an early influence upon **St Augustine** and **Gnosticism**, but the murder of Neoplatonist philosopher **Hypatia of Alexandria** (c. 350–370 AD) by **Christian zealots** seems to mark a turning point, and with the **rise of Christian orthodoxy** its influence was eventually **forced underground**. From there, it can be traced through the **Sufi branch of Islam**, the **Kabbalah of medieval Jewish mysticism**, until its gradual **re-emergence** in the **Renaissance philosophy** of **Marsilio Ficino** and **Giordano Bruno**, along the way infusing **art** and **literature**, from **Botticelli** to **Michelangelo**, and **Dante** to **Shakespeare**.

CHRISTIAN PHILOSOPHY

Christianity has always had an uneasy relationship with philosophy, and whether there can be such a thing as Christian philosophy is an intriguing question.

 NAME BOËTHIUS

 DATES C. 475–C. 526

 NATIONALITY ROMAN

 SCHOOL NEOPLATONISM

 MAIN WORKS *THE CONSOLATION OF PHILOSOPHY*

 KEY CONTRIBUTIONS ETHICS, METAPHYSICS, PHILOSOPHY OF RELIGION

SECULAR VS RELIGIOUS

From **Plato** and **Aristotle**, right through to **Bacon** and **Descartes**, and the **rise of science**, philosophy has mostly been **informed by some form of religious conviction**, and only in relatively **recent times** has it **freed itself** to become an **independent, mainly secular enterprise**.

TENSION

"**Christian philosophy**" would therefore seem an **inherent contradiction**. Christianity aims at **salvation**, where **reason falls short** and must be **bolstered by faith**. Philosophy aims at **knowledge**, utilizing **radical doubt** and **questioning**, where **no belief is sacred**. How **can these two coexist**? A Christian might also be a philosopher (as long as **philosophical conclusions did not contravene fundamental tenets of faith**), but not perhaps a philosopher in the **truest, deepest sense** – a situation exemplified, perhaps, in the **difference between theology** and **philosophy of religion**.

BOËTHIUS

Of particular interest in relation to this question is the work of **Anicius Manlius Severinus Boëthius**, better known simply as Boëthius. A Roman statesman and philosopher, he fell foul of court politics and was **imprisoned** and **executed** by **Theodric the Great** on charges of **conspiracy**. While incarcerated, he wrote ***The Consolation of Philosophy***, a hugely popular work that argues that **happiness** and **faith in God** are **still possible** in a world where **injustice** and **evil persist**. The work blends Boëthius's deep knowledge of **Greek philosophy** with **Christian principles**, but in a way that **neither evokes religious dogmas nor contravenes them**. In this respect, it perhaps comes **closest to a work of Christian philosophy**.

ZEN

Zen Buddhism shuns traditional philosophical speculation in favour of practices that attempt to help the practitioner realize his true nature.

 NAME BODHIDHARMA

 DATES FL. SIXTH TO FIFTH CENTURY AD

 NATIONALITY INDIAN

 SCHOOL BUDDHIST (CHAN)

 MAIN WORKS *TWO ENTRANCES AND FOUR PRACTICES*

 KEY CONTRIBUTIONS ETHICS, EPISTEMOLOGY

CHAN

Zen is the Japanese word for **Chan**, a **Chinese school of Mahayana Buddhism** that is said to have **originated with Bodhidharma**, an **Indian monk** who was the **first to bring Buddhism to China**. Bodhidharma is considered the **twenty-eighth** *Patriarch* of Buddhism, a **lineage of teachers** that is said to **stretch back to the Buddha himself**.

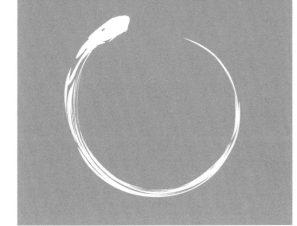

SATORI

A **central purpose of Buddhism** is to help its practitioners achieve **enlightenment** or *Satori* (to use the Japanese term), a sudden **realization of one's true nature** that **liberates one** from the **false notions** and desires that **bind us** to the **wheel of rebirth**. But since **thought itself** is **an obstacle to this realization**, Zen seeks to **bypass** or **disrupt** our **tendency to rationalize our way towards this realization** by presenting the mind with **insoluble questions** or *koans*.

THE KOAN

These **paradoxes** often take the form of **puzzles** or **riddles** – "What is the **sound of one hand clapping**?", "What **face** did you have **before you were born**?" – but a **Zen master** might employ **any means** to **shake their students** from their **habitual patterns of thought and behaviour**: **shouting, striking, shocking, behaving inappropriately or bizarrely**. The reason for this is that the **realization aimed for** – our **true nature** – is something that, in a sense, we **already know**. The question then is not, "**How do we achieve it?**", but rather, "**Why have we forgotten it?**" It is almost as if our thoughts have **lulled us asleep**. Zen tries to **wake us up**.

ISLAMIC PHILOSOPHY

When Caliph Al-Mansur (714–775) made Baghdad the capital of the new Abbasid Caliphate, he founded a city that would go on to rival Athens and Alexandria as a centre of learning and culture.

 NAME IBN RUSHD (AVERROES)

 DATES 1126–98

 NATIONALITY SPANISH MUSLIM

 SCHOOL ARISTOTELIANISM

 MAIN WORKS *THE INCOHERENCE OF INCOHERENCE*

 KEY CONTRIBUTIONS PHILOSOPHY OF RELIGION

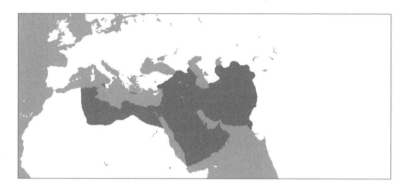

THE GOLDEN AGE

As the **Islamic Empire** grew, conquering other lands, it assimilated **Greek**, **Indian**, **Chinese**, and **Egyptian cultural influences**, creating an **Islamic Golden Age** that would see a flourishing of **art**, **science**, and **philosophy** that would span **five centuries**.

THE HOUSE OF WISDOM

The centre of this was the **House of Wisdom**, **part library** and **part academy**, **collating** and **translating scientific** and **philosophical texts** that included the works of such philosophers as **Plato**, **Aristotle**, and **Plotinus**. **Islamic philosophy** of this period is therefore often concerned with how best to blend the **rational influence** of **Aristotelianism** and **Neoplatonism** with the teachings of the **Qur'an**.

AVERROES

Foremost of the philosophers of this period is **Ibn Rushd**, better known in the West as **Averroes**. A polymath who also pursued interests in **astronomy**, **physics**, **medicine**, and even **poetry**, he was greatly influenced by **Aristotle**, writing **numerous scholarly commentaries on his works**. In this, he **moved Islamic philosophy away** from the **Neoplatonism** of **Ibn Sina**, or **Avicenna** (c. 980–1037), believing that **religion** and **philosophy** should **complement one another**, and that the truths of **faith** and **reason** were **not at odds**.

THE FLOATING MAN

Averroes' most famous **thought experiment** – the "**Floating Man**" – was intended to prove the **existence of the soul**. Somewhat **prefiguring Descartes** (discussed later), he asks us to **imagine ourselves without any senses**, any **bodily sensations at all** – **would we not still exist?**

 MEDIEVAL AND RENAISSANCE PHILOSOPHY

THE ONTOLOGICAL ARGUMENT

While other philosophers attempted to argue for God's role in the nature and existence of the world, Anselm ingeniously suggested that the best proof lay in the idea of God himself.

 NAME ST ANSELM OF CANTERBURY

 DATES 1033–1109

 NATIONALITY ITALIAN

 SCHOOL SCHOLASTICISM

 MAIN WORKS *PROSLOGION*

 KEY CONTRIBUTIONS PHILOSOPHY OF RELIGION

THE GREATEST BEING

St Anselm was an Italian-born **Christian theologian** who rose to become **Archbishop of Canterbury**. He is most remembered for his ***Proslogion***, in which he originated the **ontological argument for the existence of God**. Imagine, Anselm says, that there exists a **being no greater than which can be conceived**. If such a being existed **only in the mind**, it would be **possible to conceive** of an **even greater being** that existed both **in the mind *and* in actuality**. The French philosopher **René Descartes** (1596–1650) would later tweak this argument by **replacing greatness** with perfection, but the point is the same: such a great or perfect being (i.e. God) **must in fact exist**.

GAUNILO'S ISLAND

A famous **objection to Anselm's argument** was put forward by the French Benedictine monk **Gaunilo of Marmoutiers** (fl. eleventh century). Imagine, he says, that we replace "a **being no greater** than which can be conceived" with "a **lost island** no greater than which can be conceived". Doesn't this show the **absurdity of arguing from the supposed properties of mere ideas to actual existence**?

KANT'S PREDICATES

The German philosopher **Immanuel Kant** (1724–1804) presented a **more technical objection**. **Existence**, he said, is **not a predicate** (**quality**) something **possesses**. To say, "**God is wise**" is different to saying, "**God exists**", because "**wisdom**" is a **property an object possesses *if* it exists**.

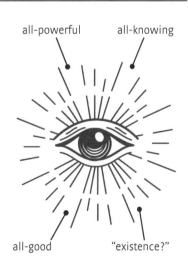

all-powerful   all-knowing

all-good   "existence?"

SCHOLASTICISM

Scholasticism was a philosophical approach that dominated the Middle Ages, attempting to blend aspects of Greek philosophy with Christian theology. Its key thinker was St Thomas Aquinas.

 NAME ST THOMAS AQUINAS

 DATES 1225–74

 NATIONALITY ITALIAN

 SCHOOL SCHOLASTICISM

 MAIN WORKS *SUMMA THEOLOGIAE; SUMMA CONTRA GENTILES*

 KEY CONTRIBUTIONS PHILOSOPHY OF RELIGION, ETHICS, METAPHYSICS, EPISTEMOLOGY

MEDIEVAL MONASTERIES

As the name implies, Scholasticism arose from the **schools** and **educational activities** associated with **Christian medieval monasteries**. As such, it is a **system** and **method** shaped and limited by the **dogmas** of the **Catholic faith**. Nonetheless, **scholastics** did much to **advance philosophical** and **scientific knowledge**, and **Aquinas** himself **defended** and **championed rational thought** against the **then prevalent view** that **reason** was a solely **corrupting influence upon religious faith**.

NATURAL THEOLOGY

Aquinas had great respect for **Aristotle**, and much of his work can be seen as an attempt to show that many aspects of the Greek philosopher's thought are **compatible with Christian scripture**. This was because, Aquinas argued, **reason itself** was a **divinely created faculty**, and so – if **guided aright** – it could **lead us not away from God**, but in fact to a **closer understanding of his creation**. Such an approach, which saw reason as providing a **bolster to faith**, has become known as *natural theology*.

EPICYCLES

However, with the growth of **science** from **Renaissance** times, "scholasticism" increasingly denoted an **inflexible approach** concerned with **fruitless** and **nit-picking controversies**. This is somewhat **unfair**, as it made many **valuable philosophical contributions**, but it's certainly true that thinkers such as **Bacon**, **Descartes**, and **Galileo** saw **scholastic dogma** as representing the **chief obstacle to progress**. For example, constrained by the **Church's assertion** – in response to **new findings** regarding **planetary movements** – that the **Earth** was the **centre of the universe**, **medieval astronomers** were forced into **increasingly complex theories** whereby **each planet moved** in its own **mini-orbit (*epicycle*)**.

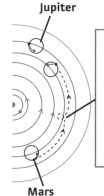

Jupiter

Epicycles helped explain the apparent *retrograde* (backwards) motion of planets.

Mars

THE COSMOLOGICAL ARGUMENT

In line with his belief that reason could reinforce faith, Aquinas originated and developed various arguments for the existence of God, among which was the cosmological argument.

CAUSE AND EFFECT

Developing ideas he found in **Plato** and **Aristotle**, **Aquinas** argued that, aside from any **particular feature it might possess**, the **existence of the universe** itself was **proof of God's existence**. This is because of the **nature of cause and effect**. If **everything that exists** has an ***efficient cause*** (to use Aristotle's term), then this **must also be true of the world itself**. The world therefore **must have a creator**, or some force that **brought it into existence**.

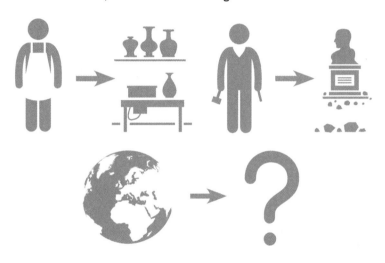

THE UNCAUSED CAUSE

But if the world itself **must have a cause**, then **what caused or created *that***? If some **physical process** or **event** brought the **universe into being**, then *that* would also seem to **require a cause**. It would appear, then, that this **potentially infinite chain of causation** must come to a **stop somewhere**, for otherwise **how would anything start**? There must therefore be some **ultimate cause** that is **responsible for creating everything** and **setting it in motion** (what Aristotle termed a "**prime mover**"), but which itself is **uncreated** or "**unmoved**". Such a **universal cause**, Aquinas argued, must be **all-powerful**, and therefore can only be God.

CAUSA SUI

But **is this the case**? Why, for instance, couldn't it be true that the world **simply popped into existence**, or was its **own cause** (***causa sui***, to use the Latin phrase)? However, Aquinas **rules this out**, for not only must all things have a cause (and **"nothing" cannot cause anything**), but a thing **cannot be its own cause**, since logically it would **have to exist before it existed** in order to **bring itself into existence**!

OCKHAM'S RAZOR

In deciding between competing theories, the English friar William of Ockham argued that the simplest explanation was often the best.

 NAME WILLIAM OF OCKHAM

 DATES 1285–1347

 NATIONALITY ENGLISH

 SCHOOL SCHOLASTICISM

 MAIN WORKS *SUMMA LOGICAE*

 KEY CONTRIBUTIONS METAPHYSICS, EPISTEMOLOGY

PRINCIPLE OF PARSIMONY

Ockham's razor, as it has become known, is a handy **rule-of-thumb**, and especially useful in cases of **scientific controversy**. It provides a **simple basis** on which to **decide between alternative explanations. All other things being equal**, it argues, we **should favour the approach that assumes the least**. For this reason, it is also known as the ***principle of parsimony***.

COMPETING THEORIES

But "**the least**" in **what sense**? Ockham's target here is ***metaphysics***, or the **nature of the world** as it exists **beyond the capacity of sense experience or logic to prove**. Because of this, **metaphysical questions** are **often impossible to resolve**. Controversies such as **who or what created the universe**, or what is the **true nature of consciousness**, persist because – **no matter what the evidence** or generally favoured **theory** – there is always a **possibility that a different approach may also fit the facts**.

METAPHYSICAL MINIMALISM

So, applying Ockham's razor, a **physicist** might argue that the **Big Bang** is the **best explanation of how the world was created** (as opposed to **God**), because a **universe driven only by physical laws** *requires **less*** in **metaphysical terms** – it is more ***minimalist***. And if we can **explain the cosmos** ***without*** God, then we **should do so**. Of course, it should be pointed out, the **assumption that true scientific explanations are simpler** is itself a **metaphysical assumption** – and therefore one that **cannot be proven**.

HUMANISM

Beginning in the fourteenth century, humanism gave human values, experiences, and concerns central importance, placing greater reliance on reason at the expense of faith or tradition.

 NAME ERASMUS

 DATES C. 1466–1536

 NATIONALITY DUTCH

 SCHOOL RENAISSANCE HUMANISM

 MAIN WORKS *IN PRAISE OF FOLLY*

 KEY CONTRIBUTIONS ETHICS, PHILOSOPHY OF RELIGION

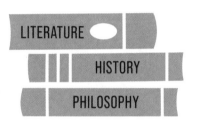

LITERATURE

HISTORY

PHILOSOPHY

RENAISSANCE

The movement has its origins in the **Renaissance Humanism** of such thinkers as **Desiderius Erasmus Roterodamus**, better known simply as **Erasmus**. A Dutch Christian scholar, Erasmus **highlighted** and **satirized** the **abuses** of the **Catholic Church**, encouraging a **rational** and **critical engagement** with **scripture**. Key to this approach was an emphasis on **education**, especially the "**humanities**" – history, **moral philosophy**, the **literature** of **Greece** and **Rome** – subjects that **literally study humanity** and its **products**, and **from which the term "humanist" derives**.

ENLIGHTENMENT

From the seventeenth to nineteenth centuries, a period commonly known as the **Enlightenment** or **Age of Reason**, philosophers such as **Voltaire**, **Hume**, and **Kant**, while **differing in certain respects** (e.g. their **attitude to religion**), nonetheless **continued** and **extended** the **humanist tradition**, emphasizing the **power** and **correct use of reason** in **science**, **philosophy**, and the **conduct of human affairs**. It is this emphasis on **reason** and **human values**, and the **importance** and **rights** of the **individual**, that eventually **developed humanism away from its religious roots** towards **secularism**.

SECULARISM

Modern or **secular humanism** generally **denies a role to religion in human affairs**, dismissing **religious claims** and preferring instead to see **humans** as the **source of meaning** and **morality**. Even philosophers who are **critical of this possibility** – such as French philosopher **Jean-Paul Sartre** – nonetheless admit that we **owe a debt to humanism** for helping us to **recognize that we cannot but see the world in human terms**. We live, in a sense, in a **human universe**, seen through the **filter** of our **own limited faculties** and **concerns**.

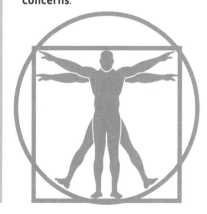

REALPOLITIK

Niccolò Machiavelli argued that political rulers should be guided not by ethical but by pragmatic concerns, in pursuit of which almost any means were justified.

 NAME NICCOLÒ MACHIAVELLI

 DATES 1469–1527

 NATIONALITY ITALIAN

 SCHOOL CLASSICAL REALISM

 MAIN WORKS *THE PRINCE*

 KEY CONTRIBUTIONS POLITICAL PHILOSOPHY

MACHIAVELLIAN

To be **Machiavellian**, in the **modern sense**, is to engage in **underhanded dealing**, **back-stabbing**, and generally **despicable scheming**. Whether Machiavelli would have been proud of this legacy is difficult to say, as **his own moral views remain debated** and **obscure**. However, it's safe to say that – in the **political arena**, at least – Machiavelli argued that the **ends often justify the means**, and that a **leader who attempts to apply Christian moral principles** is **likely to have a very short tenure**.

HUMAN NATURE

Machiavelli's philosophy may be seen as the **forerunner** of *classical realism*, or *realpolitik*, which generally concerns **international relations between countries**. Later developed by **Thomas Hobbes**, the view has **flourished in modern times**, and can be seen for instance in the *gunboat diplomacy* of **colonial empires** and the *power politics* of **Cold War superpowers**. The **underlying assumption** here is that **human nature does not change**: people will **always act** in their **self-interest**, even if this is **at your expense**. So, as **President Theodore Roosevelt** (1858–1919) put it, the **best foreign policy** is to "**speak softly and carry a big stick**".

IDEALISM

This view is generally contrasted with **political *idealism***, which argues that **international relations** are better advanced through **discussion**, **cooperation**, and the **establishment of international law**. The creation of the **United Nations** and the development of **international conventions on human rights** may therefore be seen as **examples of idealistic foreign policy**, and **evidence** of a **more trusting**, **optimistic view of human nature**.

UTOPIA

In myth, philosophy, and religion, the concept of a perfect society has existed from the earliest times, but it has increasingly taken a technological form.

 NAME SIR THOMAS MORE

 DATES 1478–1535

 NATIONALITY ENGLISH

 SCHOOL HUMANISM

 MAIN WORKS *UTOPIA*

 KEY CONTRIBUTIONS POLITICAL PHILOSOPHY

THE PERFECT ISLAND

The term *utopia* was coined by English lawyer and statesman **Sir Thomas More**, whose **1516 work of that name** – part satire and part visionary tale – pictured a **perfect island society** free from **religious intolerance**, **corruption**, and **inequality**.

DYSTOPIAS

In proposing **political** and **pragmatic solutions** to **typical human problems**, More continues a tradition begun by **Plato**, and which with the **growth of science** – from **Francis Bacon's *New Atlantis*** (1527) to **B. F. Skinner's *Walden Two*** (1948) – has increasingly seen **technology as playing a central role**. But just as technology may be used for **good** or **ill**, others have recognized a **dark side to utopia** – **communist totalitarianism** (**George Orwell's *Nineteen Eighty-Four***), pleasure-fuelled escapism (**Aldous Huxley's *Brave New World***) – and suggested that such dreams of **unachievable perfection** are as likely to result in **dystopic nightmares**.

NON-SECULAR COMMUNISM

More's islanders live a fairly simple, **communal life**, where both men and women choose from among the same range of **essential trades** (farming, weaving, carpentry, soldiering, etc.). There is **no private property** and therefore **no need of money**. As with **Plato**, **potential rulers** and **priests** are **picked out when young** to receive **special education**. There are **slaves**, but these mainly consist of **prisoners of war** and **criminals**, those who **reform** becoming eligible for **liberation**. As a result of these measures, there is **no unemployment**, **little crime**, and no **class-based resentment**. There is also **religious tolerance** for all manner of beliefs (even, to an extent, **atheism**) – which is interesting, given More's fierce opposition to the Reformation and his alleged persecution of Protestants.

SCEPTICISM

In questioning our claims to knowledge, many philosophers have considered scepticism an obstacle to be overcome, but it has also frequently played more positive roles.

NAME MICHEL DE MONTAIGNE

DATES 1533–92

NATIONALITY FRENCH

SCHOOL HUMANISM

MAIN WORKS *ESSAYS*

KEY CONTRIBUTIONS EPISTEMOLOGY, ETHICS

DEGREES OF SCEPTICISM

There are **different degrees of scepticism**. **Extreme forms** may question that existence has any **inherent meaning** (**nihilism**), that there's such a thing as **objective truth** (**relativism**), or even that **others apart from myself exist** (**solipsism**). But **such doubt is as old as philosophy itself**, and from the very beginning – citing such things as **optical illusions**, **hallucinations**, **dreams**, **lapses in memory** and **judgement** – philosophers have not been shy in highlighting what forms such doubts might take.

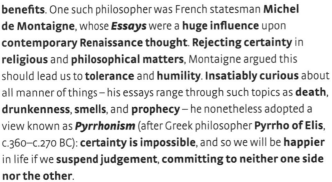

PYRRHONISM

Yet other philosophers have argued that a **general scepticism has healthy benefits**. One such philosopher was French statesman **Michel de Montaigne**, whose *Essays* were a **huge influence** upon contemporary Renaissance thought. **Rejecting certainty** in **religious** and **philosophical matters**, Montaigne argued this should lead us to **tolerance** and **humility**. **Insatiably curious** about all manner of things – his essays range through such topics as **death**, **drunkenness**, **smells**, and **prophecy** – he nonetheless adopted a view known as *Pyrrhonism* (after Greek philosopher **Pyrrho of Elis**, c.360–c.270 BC): **certainty is impossible**, and so we will be **happier** in life if we **suspend judgement**, **committing to neither one side nor the other**.

SPECIFIC DOUBT

Mostly, however, philosophers have used **weaker versions of scepticism** to support **alternative theories**. As discussed elsewhere, **Berkeley** questioned the **existence of physical matter** in support of his own brand of *idealism*; **Hume** doubted our ability to know **cause and effect independent of experience**; while **Descartes** used sceptical arguments to seek something *beyond* doubt.

THE SCIENTIFIC METHOD

The Elizabethan philosopher, lawyer and statesman Sir Francis Bacon laid the foundations for modern science by arguing that scientists must question accepted religious and philosophical authority.

 NAME SIR FRANCIS BACON

 DATES 1561–1626

 NATIONALITY ENGLISH

 SCHOOL EMPIRICISM

 MAIN WORKS *NOVUM ORGANUM; THE ADVANCEMENT OF LEARNING*

 KEY CONTRIBUTIONS PHILOSOPHY OF SCIENCE, EPISTEMOLOGY

FATHER OF THE SCIENTIFIC METHOD

Bacon is often considered the **philosophical father of modern science**. This isn't so much because scientists now follow his prescribed method, but because his approach recognized that **if scientific knowledge were to grow**, there **needed to be a greater emphasis on observation**, **experiment**, and **data collection**, and **less reliance on** the **authority of the Bible** and the **teachings of Aristotle**.

DEDUCTIVE METHOD

Aristotle's method relied largely on **logical deduction**, a process that **argues from assumptions or premises to conclusions**. If your assumptions are **correct**, and the form of your argument follows the rules of **logic** (is **valid**), then your **conclusion will be true and certain**. But if one of your premises is **false**, then, **even if the argument is valid**, the **conclusion cannot be true**. **Deductive arguments** are therefore **only as sound as the premises they are based on**, and many of **Aristotle's assumptions** – that **heavier objects fall faster than lighter ones**, that the **Earth is the centre of an eternal universe**, that **all living things keep the same form over time** – are **now disproven**.

BACON'S NEW INDUCTION

Bacon recognized that **to avoid such errors** we need to be much more **careful in advancing explanations and forming hypotheses**, a process known as *induction*. He therefore proposed a method he termed *new induction*, which focused on **amassing and comparing data**, **advancing conclusions warily and provisionally** in a way that they could be **tested by further** experiment and analysis. Unlike deduction, induction argues *beyond* what can be deduced from the premises. As such, an **inductive argument may conceivably be wrong**. However, this is the most **scientifically useful and informative type of argument**, as it **allows us to form generalizations and make predictions**.

KEY: P = PREMISE   C = CONCLUSION

A DEDUCTIVE ARGUMENT

P1: All humans eventually die.

↓

P2: Francis is human.

↓

C: Therefore Francis will eventually die.

AN INDUCTIVE ARGUMENT

P1: No human has ever lived over 200 years.

↓

C: No human will ever live beyond 200 years.

THE STATE OF NATURE

For Thomas Hobbes, the justification of political authority lay in the protection of individual rights and security, without which there would be anarchy and violence.

 NAME THOMAS HOBBES

 DATES 1588–1679

 NATIONALITY ENGLISH

 SCHOOL EMPIRICISM

 MAIN WORKS *LEVIATHAN*

 KEY CONTRIBUTIONS POLITICAL PHILOSOPHY

EARLY MODERN PHILOSOPHY

THE SOCIAL CONTRACT

What philosophers have termed the **state of nature** describes a **hypothetical situation** in which **individuals live without laws or political authority**.

Such a state may be **contrasted with** the **benefits and protections** granted members of society by **political authority**. **Relinquishing certain freedoms**, and agreeing to **abide by its laws**, society's members enter into a form of **social contract**.

A HYPOTHETICAL AGREEMENT

This contract is also **hypothetical – newborns do not read or sign anything**, and **few adults** are even **aware** of being **bound by any such agreement** – representing a **theoretical justification of political authority**. Why must we **obey laws** and **submit to the authority of the state**? Because, in return, our **rights are guaranteed** and our **security ensured** (theoretically…).

HUMAN NATURE

While many philosophers have shared this approach, they have tended to **differ on their view of human nature**, the **limits of authority**, and the **rights and freedoms** that the **social contract protects**. Among these, **Hobbes's view** is particularly **notable for its bleakness**, considering **humans** to be **inherently selfish** and **prone to violence**.

LEVIATHAN

It is to **combat** these qualities that he pictures his **ideal state** as possessing **absolute sovereignty** and **power** over its members. Like the **Leviathan**, the **mythological monster** from the biblical **Book of Job** (after which he named his political treatise), the **state** is **monstrous** and **powerful**. The state's **power** stems from all the individuals that compose it, and to **protect each other** from the **violence and anarchy inherent in our own hearts**, any **means** and **measures** appear **justified**.

CERTAINTY

*Although scepticism has long haunted philosophy, the French philosopher and scientist
René Descartes proposed that there must be a limit to those things we can doubt.*

DOUBTING THE SENSES

As most of us will acknowledge, our **senses can play tricks on us** – **optical illusions**, **mirages**, and other **sensory errors** teach us that the **information we receive through the senses** is **not always trustworthy**.

NAME RENÉ DESCARTES		**SCHOOL** RATIONALISM
DATES 1596–1650		**MAIN WORKS** *MEDITATIONS; DISCOURSE ON METHOD*
NATIONALITY FRENCH		**KEY CONTRIBUTIONS** PHILOSOPHY OF MIND, EPISTEMOLOGY

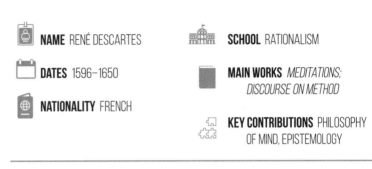

Sensory illusions   Life is a dream   Cosmic deception

WAVES OF DOUBT

But that is not the only problem. What if we were to entertain more **radical doubts**? What if you are **dreaming** this very moment, and **don't know it**? Can you be ***absolutely*** **sure** that you aren't? And what if, even more radically, the **whole of existence** is some sort of **cosmic deception** perpetrated by some **all-powerful malignant entity**, who is even capable of **tricking you as to the truth of the things you thought you were most clear about** (such as **mathematical and logical truths**)? Is it therefore **impossible to be certain about anything**?

RENÉ DESCARTES

Descartes' **key insight** was to recognize that, even faced with the **most radical doubts**, we **can at least be sure that we exist**; hence, his most famous assertion: "**I think, therefore I am**" (a statement popularly known as the ***Cogito***, after the Latin for this phrase, "***Cogito ergo sum***"). For even if everything is an **illusion**, we must at least exist ***in order to be*** deluded. And it is this **alleged certainty** (his own existence) that Descartes attempts to use as a **foundation for all knowledge**. This approach to knowledge has therefore become known as ***foundationalism***.

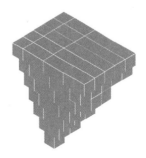

RATIONALISM

Descartes' approach to the philosophical question of how we acquire and justify what we know is termed rationalism, which argues that reason is the basis of all our knowledge.

RATIONALISM VS EMPIRICISM

Historically, there are **two main approaches** to *epistemology* (the **theory of knowledge**): *rationalism* and *empiricism*. **Empiricists** argue that **most or even all** of our knowledge comes from **experience**, while **rationalists** argue that **rational ideas** play the **central role**. The terms now have mostly a **historical sense**, and philosophers may display traits from both, though these labels are still helpful in understanding how these **two schools** have **shaped the course of philosophy**.

NOTABLE RATIONALISTS

René Descartes (1596–1650)
Baruch Spinoza (1632–77)
Gottfried Leibniz (1646–1716)

NOTABLE EMPIRICISTS

John Locke (1632–1704)
Bishop Berkeley (1685–1753)
David Hume (1711–76)

INNATE IDEAS

As a rationalist, Descartes argued that while **sense experience** played an important role in **presenting us with information**, such experience was **meaningless without a framework of rational ideas** within which **to understand** and **interpret it**. Like **Plato**, Descartes believed that many of these rational ideas were present **from birth** (**innate**), and were only "**drawn out**" by **experience**. Unlike **vague** sense impressions, the best rational ideas were "**clear and distinct**", and the **degree to which this was so** indicated **how likely they were to be true** (the most "clear and distinct" idea being the *Cogito*).

DESCARTES' CANDLE

To illustrate his point, Descartes used the example of a **candle**: in its **normal state**, it has **certain properties** (**shape**, **smell**, **colour**, **weight**, **size**, etc.), but once it **melts**, these qualities **change**. What, then, are the candle's **"real" properties**? We can only understand them in **scientific terms** – the way the **wax melts** as the **heat breaks down the molecular bonds**, the way the **colour changes** as the **light interacts differently on the translucent wax**. The **true understanding** of the nature of the wax candle is therefore **dependent on fundamental rational ideas** and **scientific principles**, and not (or **not just**) the **experience** that our **senses provide us**.

- unmelted candle
- red
- tall
- cylindrical

v

- melted candle
- soft
- smaller

DESCARTES' DREAM

Despite its apparently **scientific basis**, Descartes' **rationalism** seems to have had a **religious inspiration**. As a young man staying in a little village in Bavaria, Descartes had a **religious experience**. Huddled in a walled stove against the cold, he experienced three unsettling **waking dreams** or **visions** (similar to his **"waves of doubt"**), which would shape his **eventual conviction** that the **universe** was **rationally ordered** and could be **understood through the application of human reason**.

DUALISM

Having concluded that we are essentially mental beings, Descartes divides human nature into two fundamentally different substances, a view known as dualism.

TWO SUBSTANCES

Following his arrival at the **ultimate certainty** (the ***Cogito***), **Descartes** concludes that we are essentially "**thinking things**". I may **walk** and **talk**, eat and **sleep**, but my **essential self**, which **cannot be doubted**, is **mental**. In contrast, my **body** is **less easily known**; it's conceivable that **"I" could continue to exist without it**, and **its existence may even be doubted**. ***Cartesian dualism*** therefore argues that we possess a **body** made of **physical stuff** (***res extensa***), and a **mind** made of **mental stuff** (***res cogitans***). Mind, for Descartes, has **no physical properties**; it does not take up **space** or possess any **moving parts** – in fact, it has **no parts at all**. In contrast, physical things have no **mental properties**; they do not **think** or **feel**, **sense** or **desire** (in any **conscious manner**), all such things being the **province of mind**.

Matter (*res extensa* – Latin for "extended thing"): unthinking, unfeeling; possessing dimensions in space (size, shape, mass); can be measured, can be divided.

Mind (*res cogitans* – Latin for "thinking thing"): thinking, feeling; possessing no size, shape or mass; not measurable or divisible.

THE PROBLEM OF INTERACTION

But if these substances are so radically different, **how do they interact**? How do we **control our bodies**, or **interpret physical sensations**? This has become known as the ***problem of interaction***, which, as Descartes' contemporaries were first to point out, would seem to have **no easy solution**, for **either mind and matter cannot by definition interact**, or else they are **not so distinct as Descartes supposed** – and if so, **why should we think of there being two separate "substances"?** Descartes seemed not to recognize the seriousness of this problem, and his own **proposed solutions** are **tentative** and **half-thought-out**. For instance, he suggested that interaction might take place **via the pineal gland in the brain** – but isn't this ... **physical**? Which just **restates the problem**.

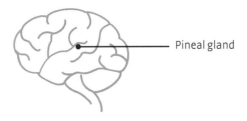

Pineal gland

POSSIBLE SOLUTIONS

Because of this problem, **most later philosophers** have **abandoned dualism** in favour of some form of ***physical monism*** (the idea that there is **only one substance**, and it is **physical**, not **mental**). Of course, as we'll see later, this causes **other problems**.

THE TRADEMARK ARGUMENT

To guarantee knowledge, Descartes needed to prove the existence of God. One argument he advanced pointed to the evidence provided by the existence of the idea of God in our minds.

THE DIVINE CRAFTSMAN

In addition to providing a **variation of the ontological argument** advanced by **St Anselm**, Descartes argued that the fact that we even have an **idea of God** was itself **significant**. While the ontological argument attempts to argue from the **nature of the idea of a perfect being** that **such a being must exist**, the **trademark argument** proposes that the **very existence of the idea of God** is **proof that he himself must have put it in our minds**, rather like the **signature** or **trademark** of a **craftsman** upon his **finished work**.

THE CARTESIAN CIRCLE

Notoriously, however, Descartes' **attempts to guarantee knowledge** led him into what appears to be a **circular argument**. We know **certain ideas are true** because they are "**clear and distinct**". But **how can we trust** that "clear and distinct" ideas are true? Because, Descartes argues, God, who created him, is *not* **malevolent**, and wouldn't allow what we "**clearly and distinctly perceive**" to be **false**. But how do we know God exists? Because we clearly and distinctly perceive the **truth of arguments for his existence**... And so, the argument is circular: he **needs God to guarantee clear and distinct ideas**, and **clear and distinct ideas to prove God exists**.

THE ORIGIN OF IDEAS

But ideas can come from **anywhere**. Perhaps the idea of God has **some other source**? Could Descartes have acquired it through his **own experience**, or perhaps via his **imagination**? Can we, though, ever get a true idea of **omnipotence** by (for instance) taking **everyday examples of power** and **amplifying them**? Or of **omniscience**, by taking the **intelligence of a wise person** and **multiplying it**? Wouldn't that only give us a being *more* intelligent or capable, not something *infinitely* wise or powerful? If so, such ideas **cannot come from experience**, and must therefore be *innate*, **left in our minds by God**, who is the **only being powerful and wise enough to have originated them**. Descartes' argument therefore relies on the notion that we can **never acquire a true idea of infinity** (or omniscience, or omnipotence) **via experience**. But is he right? We cannot draw **two lines that go on forever**, never meeting, but can't we *suggest* this idea?

PASCAL'S WAGER

Rejecting conventional arguments for the existence of God as inconclusive, Pascal argued that, given what is at stake and the cost of losing, belief in God represents the "best bet".

 NAME BLAISE PASCAL

 DATES 1623–62

 NATIONALITY FRENCH

 SCHOOL RATIONALISM

 MAIN WORKS *PENSÉES*

 KEY CONTRIBUTIONS PHILOSOPHY OF RELIGION

BLAISE PASCAL

French **philosopher**, **scientist**, and **mathematician Blaise Pascal** was as **religiously devout** as he was **academically brilliant**, and his two natures pulled him in **opposite directions** throughout his life. **Religion** required **faith**, **humility**, and **obedience**, whereas **science** sought **explanations**, fostered **pride** in one's abilities, and **questioned assumptions**. In fact, Pascal came to believe, **you could never use reason alone to guarantee the truth of religion**. The final step must always be a **voluntary one**.

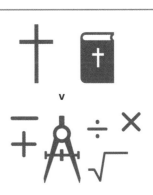

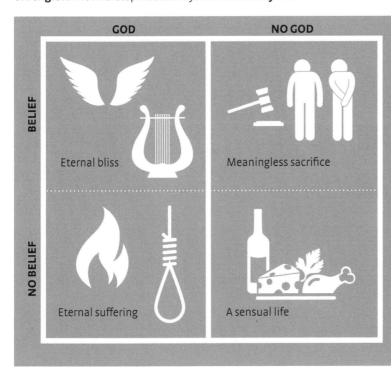

GOD / NO GOD

BELIEF — Eternal bliss / Meaningless sacrifice

NO BELIEF — Eternal suffering / A sensual life

A RATIONAL GAMBLE

However, it was **still possible to appeal to reason** in order to encourage faith. One such attempt is what has become known as **Pascal's wager**. Faced with the question of **God's existence**, and the choice of **how to spend one's life**, what is the **most rational thing to do**? An **eternity of heavenly bliss** will always outweigh a **life in pursuit of pleasure**, and **fear of eternal damnation** trumps **fear of missing out on sensual enjoyment**. Isn't it best, then, to **gamble on God** and the **virtuous life**? Just think of the pay-out!

MONISM

While Cartesian dualism raised the problem of how mind and matter interacted, Spinoza resolved this by proposing that they were in fact two aspects of the same single substance.

 NAME BARUCH SPINOZA

 DATES 1632–77

 NATIONALITY DUTCH

 SCHOOL RATIONALISM

 MAIN WORKS *ETHICS*

 KEY CONTRIBUTIONS METAPHYSICS, PHILOSOPHY OF MIND, PHILOSOPHY OF RELIGION

DIVINE UNITY

There is some debate about **Spinoza's exact views**. On the **relation of God to the physical world**, he is sometimes claimed to be a ***pantheist*** (the idea that **God is identical with Nature**), or some sort of ***panentheist*** (where **Nature is part of** but **not the totality of God**, which **extends beyond**). Whatever the case, Spinoza shares the ***monist*** view of **Parmenides** that there are **no individual substances**, and that **everything that exists** is **part of** the **same underlying unity**.

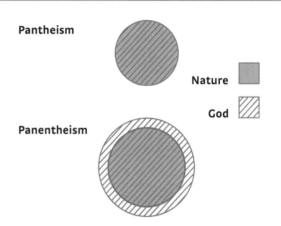

ATTRIBUTES AND MODES

Spinoza's views therefore make an **interesting contrast** with those of his **fellow rationalist Descartes**, whom he was heavily **influenced by**. However, unlike Descartes, Spinoza considers **Thought** (**mind**) and **Extension** (**matter**) to be *attributes* of God (aspects of his being), where **individual entities** are mere *modes* or modifications of these **attributes**. Descartes considered **physical things** to all be part of the **same substance** – the **atoms of my body mingle with those of the universe** in general. But for Spinoza, this was **also true of mind**: just as **individual physical things** are merely **different shapings of the same physical stuff**, so **individual minds** are modifications of the **same *mental stuff***. We are **all**, in a sense, the **thoughts of God**.

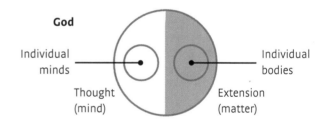

DETERMINISM

One consequence of Spinoza's **monism** is that, since we have **no independent existence**, and are mere **conduits** for the **divine attributes** of **thought** and **physical extension**, then we have **no free will**. **Everything we do** is an **expression of God's will**.

EMPIRICISM

Although not the first, John Locke was among the foremost of the British empiricists, arguing that experience played the key role in the acquisition of knowledge.

 NAME JOHN LOCKE

 DATES 1632–1704

 NATIONALITY ENGLISH

 SCHOOL EMPIRICISM

 MAIN WORKS *A LETTER CONCERNING TOLERATION; TWO TREATISES OF GOVERNMENT; AN ESSAY CONCERNING HUMAN UNDERSTANDING*

 KEY CONTRIBUTIONS METAPHYSICS, EPISTEMOLOGY, POLITICAL PHILOSOPHY, PHILOSOPHY OF MIND

TABULA RASA

Locke famously argued that **at birth** the **mind** was a ***tabula rasa*** or blank slate, **ready to receive** whatever **impressions** the **senses** would **imprint upon it**, from which it could then **build** and **test** ideas and **theories**.

SIMPLE AND COMPLEX IDEAS

The **sense impressions** that were the **foundations of knowledge** were what Locke called ***simple ideas***. These were such things as **colours**, **smells**, **tastes**, **shapes**, and so on. The **mind** then **worked on these** – **abstracting**, **comparing**, and **combining** – to form ***complex ideas***, relating to **space and time**, **cause and effect**, and other **fundamental notions**. For instance, a **sense impression** of an **orange** would generate **various simple ideas**: **orangeness**, **roundness**, roughness, and so on. The mind can then work on these to produce more **sophisticated ideas**, such as fruit or ripeness.

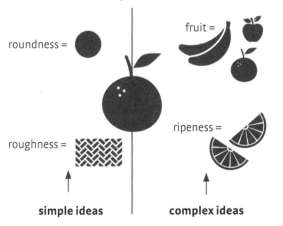

roundness =

roughness =

fruit =

ripeness =

simple ideas

complex ideas

INNATE KNOWLEDGE

In this approach, **Locke opposed the belief**, held by such **rationalists** as **Descartes**, that **certain ideas** were **innate (present from birth)**. He presented **two main lines of argument** against this. First, he noted that **human history** and **culture** were **not uniform**, suggesting that different peoples evolved **different notions and ideas** from **different experiences**. Second, he argued that any **common ideas** were **better explained** by the fact that **humans share the same mental capacities** and **types of experience**.

TOLERANCE

While European Protestants and Catholics tore each other apart over the correct interpretation of their peace-loving religion, John Locke proposed that the true way forward was tolerance.

DISESTABLISHMENT

Locke argued that there were a **number of good reasons** for a **state to foster toleration of differing religious views**. Chief of these was the fact that **human judgement** is **fallible – how can we really be certain of what God truly intended**, or **how scripture should be interpreted**? For a **society** to be **just** and **peaceful**, there should therefore be a **separation of church** and **state** (what's called ***disestablishment***), so that **laws** it **creates** and **enforces** arise **independently** of any **one set of religious convictions**, and **no state-sponsored persecution** on **religious grounds** is **possible**.

PERSONAL CONVICTION

Locke also argued that **tolerance** was likely to create a **more orderly and peaceful society**. We **cannot force someone** to truly change their beliefs, and **attempting to do** so is actually more likely to **foster opposition**. In fact, as **fellow liberal philosopher John Stuart Mill** would later argue, **freedom to express** and **discuss** a **variety of views** is more likely to create **social cohesion**, as **free debate** allows people to engage **rationally** with others and to seek to **change their own or others' views peaceably**.

THE PARADOX OF TOLERANCE

The problem with the **practice of tolerance**, however, is that it would seem to **allow for its opposite**. Should we tolerate views that are in themselves ***intolerant***? This leads to what Austrian philosopher **Karl Popper** called the ***paradox of tolerance:* unlimited tolerance** itself allows views that **undermine the practice of tolerance**. Should we therefore **set limits** to **free speech** and **action** – to what should be tolerated – such as by **criminalizing hate speech**? But **who decides where these limits are set**?

PERSONAL IDENTITY

Locke was the first to propose the view that personal identity was based on our consciousness of being the same person, with the same memories.

MORAL RESPONSIBILITY

Locke wondered what made an individual **accountable** for their **past actions**. If we're going to **blame** (or **praise**) someone for something they did **ten years ago**, we must understand **what ensures an individual's *personal identity***. What makes us the ***same person*** from day to day?

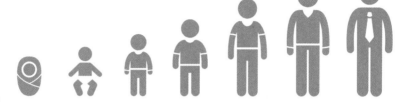

PHYSICAL CONTINUITY

With **physical objects**, **identity** was based on tracing a **line through time** from **one stage of existence to another**, showing how the **physical parts** have the **same or similar organization** and function, have **grown** and **changed over time** (or **not**). A **pup** and an **adult dog** are the **same dog** because we can see they possess **similar markings**, have **four legs**, a **tail**, like to **chase cats**, etc. So even though there is **growth** and **change in behaviour** and **appearance**, the dog's life **holds these together** in a sort of **story** determined by its **nature** and **function**.

PSYCHOLOGICAL CONTINUITY

But when we come to consider if the "John" we know **today** is the **same *person*** as the "John" **who existed ten years ago**, **continuous possession** of the **same body** isn't enough. To **prosecute** someone for a **crime**, **Locke** argued, it must be the case that they **remember *committing*** that **crime**. You might **temporarily lose mental capacity** through **drugs**, **psychosis**, or even **sleepwalking**, and – perhaps justifiably – **claim your innocence**: you simply **don't remember**. And for Locke, that was **enough to determine** that you were **not in fact the same person**. This has a number of interesting **consequences**, which we'll look at later in the book.

THE PRINCIPLE OF SUFFICIENT REASON

Leibniz believed that nothing that exists does so without a reason, that every event has a cause, and everything that was true had some justification that explained why.

 NAME GOTTFRIED WILHELM LEIBNIZ

 DATES 1646–1716

 NATIONALITY GERMAN

 SCHOOL RATIONALISM

 MAIN WORKS *DISCOURSE ON METAPHYSICS; NEW ESSAYS ON HUMAN UNDERSTANDING; THEODICY; MONADOLOGY*

 KEY CONTRIBUTIONS EPISTEMOLOGY, METAPHYSICS, PHILOSOPHY OF RELIGION

THE RATIONAL UNIVERSE

The **principle of sufficient reason** is fundamentally the idea that the **world is intelligible and rational**. **Any question** we can ask should therefore, in theory, **be capable of being answered**. Of course, we might **never find those answers** – **Leibniz** wasn't suggesting that it was **possible to know everything** – but in matters of **physics**, **logic**, or even **religion**, we can at least be sure that **such answers exist**, and that **in all the universe** there is **no element of randomness or chance**.

INFINITE REGRESS

But **explanations have to stop somewhere**. If **every reason** itself **has to have a reason**, then this **could go on forever** – what's called an **infinite regress**.

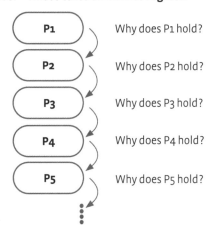

P1	Why does P1 hold?
P2	Why does P2 hold?
P3	Why does P3 hold?
P4	Why does P4 hold?
P5	Why does P5 hold?

NECESSARY TRUTHS

To avoid this, **Leibniz** argued that **certain things** were **true by necessity**. In other words, they **needed no further justification**. We know that *something* caused the noise we just heard, because of the **fundamental, necessary truth** that "every effect has a cause". But how do we know that this is true? Because it would be **self-contradictory to deny it**. For instance, if there were **some effects without causes** (the reason they happen), we would also **lose the ability to ask why this was** (to **give a reason**), and eventually the **whole thing would unravel** – to the point where we **could not ask the reason behind anything**. The **universe** would be **unintelligible**.

POSSIBLE WORLDS

In philosophy, the idea of other possible worlds has long provided a useful tool for understanding the true nature of this one.

LEIBNIZ

Leibniz famously argued that we live in the **best of all possible worlds**. By this he meant that, **no matter** what the **apparent flaws** of **this world**, and though **other worlds** were **conceivable**, **God** – in his **infinite wisdom** and **goodness** – **chose to create this one**.

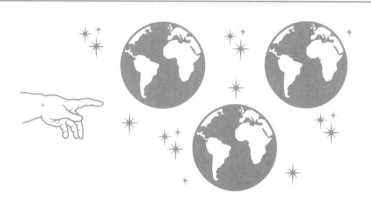

MODAL LOGIC

Since then, philosophers have used this concept in other ways. ***Modal logic*** considers a statement in relation to ***in what way*** **it might be true or false** (e.g. whether it is ***necessarily*** true, or only ***possibly so***). For instance, it's ***possible*** for there to have been a **world with flying pigs** (or pig-like things), but ***not*** where **two pigs plus two pigs equals five pigs**.

RIGID DESIGNATORS

Interestingly, as pointed out by American philosopher **Saul Kripke**, this fixes the meaning of **proper names** (what he terms ***rigid designators***), which **must denote** the **same thing** in **every possible world**. There might be **possible worlds** where **Neil Armstrong** wasn't an **astronaut** but a **basketball star**, but there are **no possible worlds** where Neil Armstrong had **different parents**, or **different genes** (though there might be others called Neil Armstrong, as there are **in this world**). This puts a **new slant** on the question of **what your life would be like** if you were born to **different parents**, were of a **different race**, or whatever: such a person **wouldn't be "you"**.

DAVID LEWIS

While **possible worlds** are **mostly used hypothetically** to **explore metaphysical questions**, American philosopher **David Lewis** argued that **such worlds do actually exist**. If we can **conceive** of **logically consistent possible worlds**, then – **wherever** and **however** they might do so – **what's to stop them from actually existing**?

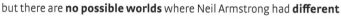

65

IDEALISM

The Irish philosopher Bishop Berkeley agreed with Locke that all ideas come from experience, but pointed out that this does not in fact give us proof that the world is physical.

EARLY MODERN PHILOSOPHY

 NAME BISHOP GEORGE BERKELEY

 DATES 1685–1753

 NATIONALITY IRISH

 SCHOOL EMPIRICISM

 MAIN WORKS *A TREATISE CONCERNING THE PRINCIPLES OF HUMAN KNOWLEDGE; THREE DIALOGUES BETWEEN HYLAS AND PHILONOUS*

 KEY CONTRIBUTIONS EPISTEMOLOGY, METAPHYSICS, PHILOSOPHY OF MIND

PRIMARY AND SECONDARY QUALITIES

For **Locke**, all objects possess **primary** and **secondary qualities**. An apple has certain **objective, physical characteristics** – size, shape, weight, etc. – and certain **subjective**, or *mind-dependent* qualities – colour, taste, texture, etc. Secondary qualities are *mind-dependent* because they **depend on conscious observers**, who **differ** as to their **relations** and **attitude** to the object (**colour** changes according to **viewpoint**; **taste** varies between individuals). In contrast, **physical properties** are **independent** (an apple either weighs 5 ounces or it doesn't, is either round or it isn't).

Primary qualities:
- round
- 4 inches diameter
- 5 ounces

Secondary qualities:
- red
- smooth
- shiny

NON-EXISTENT MATTER

This distinction was not only shared by **Locke** but also by **non-empiricists** such as **Descartes**, and **scientists** such as **Galileo** and **Newton**. But Berkeley reasoned that, **if *all* our knowledge comes from experience**, then **what is our evidence that there is a physical "stuff" that underlies all these properties**? Isn't that an **unprovable metaphysical assumption**? Aren't *all* properties of an object "**mind-dependent**"? Size is **relative**, and even **shape** depends on the **perspective of the** viewer. In fact, **all we really have evidence for** (as Descartes would partly agree) is the **mind itself**. Perhaps, then, mind *is* all that exists.

THE ROLE OF GOD

But **without assuming physical matter**, what **holds the properties of an object in one place**, ensuring that they can be **re-experienced over time** or by **different individuals**? Berkeley's answer was **God**, who ensured that all objects were **permanent *possibilities of perception*** by holding them as **ideas in his mind**.

BUSHIDŌ

Bushidō persists in the practice of Japanese martial arts, but evolved from a code of ethics that regulated the conduct of the samurai warrior.

 NAME YAMAMOTO TSUNETOMO

 DATES 1659–1719

 NATIONALITY JAPANESE

 SCHOOL BUSHIDŌ

 MAIN WORKS *HAKAGURE*

 KEY CONTRIBUTIONS ETHICS

SAMURAI CODE

Bushidō is an eclectic mix of **Chinese Confucianism**, the native **Shinto religion of Japan**, and **Zen Buddhism**. As such, it blends **courage** and **equanimity** in the **face of death** with a **strict code** of **social etiquette** and **moral obligation**. Originally a **noble warrior caste**, often serving as **retainers to feudal lords**, the samurai gradually **lost status**. With the advent of **modern warfare** their **military relevance all but disappeared**, and they were **officially abolished** in 1870.

TSUNETOMO

Bushidō may stem from embedded **oral** and **social traditions** going back centuries, but it owes its **codification** to the seventeenth-century text *Hakagure* ("Hidden Leaves") by samurai **Yamamoto Tsunetomo**. Writing at a time of peace, when the **traditional role** of the **samurai** had **already begun to decline**, Tsunetomo himself saw no military action, and later became a **monk**. The *Hakagure* may therefore be seen in part as a **nostalgic work**, celebrating an **ideal** way of **duty** and **self-sacrifice**. In this, **death is central** and **must be embraced**, shaping **life** by giving it **purity** and **purpose**, an **honourable death** being **preferable** to a **shameful life** (the usual **remedy** for which is *seppuku* or *hara-kiri*, an act of **ritual suicide**).

KAMIKAZE

Despite the **disappearance** of the **samurai** themselves, bushidō continued to permeate **Japanese military culture**, and can be seen especially in the *kamikaze* **suicide missions** of **fighter pilots** during the **Second World War**, and the **refusal of many Japanese troops to surrender** no matter what the circumstances, preferring to **fight** to the **death**.

HUME'S FORK

Like Locke and Berkeley, David Hume considered all knowledge to stem ultimately from experience, but he developed their empiricism to more radical and sceptical conclusions.

 NAME DAVID HUME

 DATES 1711–76

 NATIONALITY SCOTTISH

 SCHOOL EMPIRICISM

 MAIN WORKS *ENQUIRY CONCERNING HUMAN UNDERSTANDING; TREATISE OF HUMAN NATURE; DIALOGUES CONCERNING NATURAL RELIGION*

 KEY CONTRIBUTIONS EPISTEMOLOGY, METAPHYSICS, ETHICS, PHILOSOPHY OF RELIGION

MATTERS OF FACT

If all **knowledge** comes from **experience**, then, **Hume** argued, **all assertions fall into one of two camps**: *matters of fact* or *relations of ideas*. Dealing with the first of these first, matters of fact are those **things that we learn from experience**: Fred is **taller** than Alice, Dave's new car is **blue**, and so on. **Logic cannot teach us these things**, but we **must learn** them through **sense experience**.

Fred — taller → Alice · DAVE1

METAPHYSICAL SPECULATION

But what makes Hume's **empiricism** more **radical** is the **conclusions he draws** from this, for **if a statement does not fall into one of these two camps**, it is virtually **meaningless**. This, of course, includes large sections of the **philosophical library – ethics**, **philosophy of religion**, **metaphysics** – tomes from which he would gladly see consigned to the flames. This is not to say that Hume has nothing to say on these topics (as we shall see), but he is keen to **draw a line between** those **logical and empirical statements** that **we *can*** make, and those that represent mere **idle *metaphysical*** speculation about the **world that exists *beyond* experience and logic**.

RELATIONS OF IDEAS

In contrast, **relations of ideas** refer to the things that we **don't need to check**, because they are **true** (or **false**) by **logic alone**. If Peter is shorter than Alice, and Fred is taller than Alice, we don't need to check whether Fred is **taller** than Peter, because logic dictates that he is. If Nigel is a **bachelor**, we don't also have to check whether he has a **wife**, because bachelor means "unmarried man". And the same goes for **mathematical calculations**: no matter how many times we "check" what "2 + 2" is, the **answer will always be "4"** (though, obviously, we may make **mistakes** in counting).

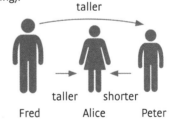

taller

Fred — taller → Alice ← shorter — Peter

$2 + 2 = 4$

Bachelor

THE IS—OUGHT GAP

In turning his sceptical empiricism to ethics, Hume argued that reason cannot teach us "right" from "wrong", but that these are things decided by the passions.

HUME'S GUILLOTINE

Just as **Hume** divided **judgements** into **relations of logic and experience**, so he also introduced a **broader distinction**, which is often called **Hume's Guillotine** or **Hume's Law**. Here he introduces a distinction between **fact** and **value**, and argues that the **facts of any situation** (what *is*) can **never determine** what we *ought* to do in relation to it. Jim steals money from John; **stealing is wrong**; therefore, we **ought to prosecute** Jim. This seems **straightforward** and **logical**. However, Hume pointed out that the **mere description of the situation** (Jim's theft) **does not** in fact **determine the outcome** (prosecution).

VALUE JUDGEMENTS

There is a sleight of hand here involving the word "**steal**", which is already a **value-laden judgement**. If we replace it with the more **neutral** word "**take**", for instance, we can see how the **trick** works: "Jim takes money from John" is a simple **statement of fact**, and we might then have a **debate** about whether the "taking" was in fact **moral** or **immoral**, **legal** or **illegal**. But this further debate is where the **values** come in, and it is their **attachment to facts** that determines whether something is "**right**" or "**wrong**". Of course, this is even clearer if we take a subject about which there is **ongoing debate** as to its **legality** – such as **abortion**, **euthanasia**, or **drug use**.

= "Jim took something from John" (fact); "Stealing is wrong" (value)

Jim stole | from John

MORAL SENTIMENTS

Hume is therefore arguing against ***moral realism*** (the view that there are such things as **moral facts**). So, does that mean that we are **free to do what we wish**? Not exactly, for we are in fact **guided** by what Hume termed ***moral sentiments***. These are **emotional responses** that we feel towards others as a result of our **common human nature**. The response of people who see a child being beaten, or a similar act of **cruelty**, will probably be similar (**outrage** or **pity**). And it is the fact that **human beings share these sentiments** that allows them to develop a **common code of ethics**. Of course, these codes may **differ** slightly between **cultures** and different **periods of history** – as in fact they do – but they allow for a **remarkably common ethical response**, and one in which **reason** plays a **secondary role**.

69

THE PROBLEM OF INDUCTION

While philosophers had long recognized that inductive arguments are less certain than deductive ones, Hume argued that this requires a completely different account of scientific knowledge.

CAUSE AND EFFECT

The **Sun rises**, **apples fall from trees**, **fire generates heat and light** – human endeavour is built on the expectation that **such occurrences will not change**. If apple farmers had to start protecting their crop from the possibility that it might go floating off into the sky, life would become very complicated and unpredictable.

CUSTOM

So is there no such thing as a **necessary connection between events**? Are the **laws of nature** potentially **random**? Hume said not. Just as **human nature fills the gap** between **what is** and **what ought to be** in our **moral world**, the gap between **cause and effect** is supplied by what Hume called **_custom_**. The fact that we **expect** an apple to fall is due to our **witnessing** the **_constant conjunction_** between (for instance) the wind blowing and the apple falling. It is therefore these constant conjunctions of events (the **Sun rising**, the **apple falling**, **fire and heat**) that allow our minds to identify the **cause–effect relationship**.

NECESSARY CONNECTION

Rationalists such as **Descartes** and **Leibniz** had assumed that there was a **_necessary connection_** between such events that guaranteed their **certainty**. As an **empiricist**, however, **Hume** argued that – rationally speaking, at least – we cannot claim such certainty. There is **no logical reason why apples should fall**. Logically, flying apples are fine, for it is not logic that teaches us that apples fall, but **experience**. And there's nothing to stop the next **experience** from **being different**. This is known as the **problem of induction**.

MENTAL ASSOCIATIONS

How do we do this? Hume seems to imply that it is an **innate ability of the mind**. Just as we **instinctively associate ideas** that bear a **common resemblance** (**ball** and **Sun**, for instance), or that are **near to one another** (thinking of "five" makes us think of "six"), so our minds look for **causal relationships**. They may occasionally be **wrong**, perhaps, but **without such an ability, there would be no science**.

THE TELEOLOGICAL ARGUMENT

Religious believers often cite the intricacy and order of the natural world as proof that the world had a creator, but even if true, Hume argued, this can tell us nothing about the designer.

INTELLIGENT DESIGN

It is not hard to be lost in wonder at the extraordinary **complexity**, **beauty**, and **variety** of the **natural world**. And so it is **easy to have sympathy for the idea** that there is an **intelligence behind it**. This is known as the *teleological argument* for **God's existence**, from the Greek word *telos*, meaning **purpose**. **Bees pollinate flowers**, **worms aerate** the **soil** to help **plants grow**, and so on; each **creature** and **organism** seems endowed with a **reason for existing**, and all **work together** in a **natural harmony**.

THE UNKNOWN CAUSE

It therefore seems **almost inconceivable** that all this **could have arisen by chance**. Modern **evolutionary theory** provides an alternative account of how this **complexity** may have arisen, but **Hume** chose a different form of attack. Since, he argued, our knowledge of **causation** is due to **experience** – from seeing the *constant conjunction* of events – how are we to gain any **knowledge** of the **creation of the world**?

ALTERNATIVE CAUSES

Even if the universe were **created**, this **doesn't prove that the designer was the God of monotheism**; judging by the **cruelty of nature**, we might just as readily assume that the deity was **evil**, **incompetent**, or **immature**, like some **divine toddler**. And, of course, we cannot **compare this universe with others**, as we might compare a stone and an ornament, to see if one shows **more signs of design**; for all we know, such **complexity might be naturally occurring**. Overall, then, while our minds are fitted to **discern causal relations** within the **natural world**, they are *not* fitted to argue **beyond experience**; from an *effect* (the **universe**) back to its *cause* (whatever that might be...). .

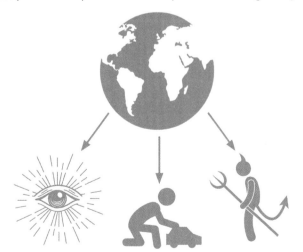

MIRACLES

Since by definition a miracle is a contravention of the laws of nature, then, given the small likelihood that such events actually happen, Hume argues that we should always prefer other explanations.

THE WEIGHT OF HISTORY

Because our **knowledge** of **natural laws** stems from **experience** and **custom**, any **contravention** of those laws has the **weight of human history** against it. If someone says that they have seen a **statue weep**, or a **terminal patient** appears to undergo a **"miraculous" recovery**, the **most likely explanation** will always be a **natural one**: there is a hole in the church roof and the statue only weeps when it rains; the patient's prognosis was too severe. Add to this that **reliable reports of miracles** seem **hard to come by**, and **witnesses** can often be ruled out as **credulous**, **superstitious**, or **biased**, then the **case for miracles seems very slim**.

DIVINE INTERVENTION

One **criticism** of Hume's position, however, is that his **definition of acceptable proof** would seem to rule out the possibility of any such proof being found. If enough **reliable witnesses** could **testify** to the **miraculous event**, and it occurred **sufficiently often** that **other factors** could be **ruled out**, what we would be witnessing would **not be a miracle at all**, but **some other little-known law of nature**. However, miracles are, traditionally, infrequent *suspensions* of the laws of nature – there **can be no "law" of miracles**, because they represent the **will of God**, who has chosen on this occasion to **intervene**. Hume's position therefore says less perhaps about miracles than it does about his **atheism**.

ROMANTICISM

Jean-Jacques Rousseau was a hugely influential figure whose reaction against the Enlightenment's emphasis upon reason and social progress became a cornerstone of Romanticism.

 NAME JEAN-JACQUES ROUSSEAU

 DATES 1712–78

 NATIONALITY GENEVAN (SWISS)

 SCHOOL ROMANTICISM

 MAIN WORKS *THE SOCIAL CONTRACT; EMILE; CONFESSIONS*

 KEY CONTRIBUTIONS POLITICAL PHILOSOPHY

EARLY MODERN PHILOSOPHY

THE ENLIGHTENMENT

While they **disagreed on how**, thinkers such as **Bacon, Descartes, Locke,** and **Hume** broadly **shared a vision** of the **improvement of human affairs** by the **rejection of tradition and authority** in favour of more **rational principles and methods**. The period during which this approach was **most influential** is known as the ***Enlightenment***, and the Swiss philosopher **Rousseau** is often considered one of its **foremost examples**. However, there are **important respects** in which Rousseau's thought went **counter to Enlightenment thinking**, and he is also considered a **founding influence on *Romanticism***.

THE NOBLE SAVAGE

In **Rousseau's philosophy**, this translates into a view of **man as naturally good**, and of **society as a necessary evil**. Like **Hobbes** and **Locke**, he favours a form of **social contract theory**, but rejects Hobbes's **pessimistic view of human nature**, arguing that it's really **society that corrupts**, and that, in a **state of nature**, **"primitive" man** was a **kindly, empathetic creature – "a noble savage"** (as this ideal was popularly described).

ROMANTICISM

The **Romantic Movement** is often associated with **poetry, music,** and **art**; with **Coleridge** and **Wordsworth**, **Beethoven** and **Wagner**, **Constable** and **Turner**. As a philosophy, it **emphasizes emotion over reason**, and **nature over "civilized" society**.

A SENTIMENTAL EDUCATION

Like **Hume, Rousseau** also emphasized the **key role of emotion** or ***sentiment*** in **moral education**, and in his philosophical novel ***Emile, or On Education***, the **final stage** of his protagonist's **ideal education** is to foster the **correct emotional attitudes**; that, having developed **physically** and **intellectually**, the **ideal individual** must also cultivate ***feeling***.

THE FREE MARKET

Adam Smith's belief in a free market, unfettered by government interference, became a cornerstone of classical liberalism.

 NAME ADAM SMITH

 DATES 1723–90

 NATIONALITY SCOTTISH

 SCHOOL LIBERALISM (EMPIRICISM)

 MAIN WORKS *THE WEALTH OF NATIONS; THE THEORY OF MORAL SENTIMENTS*

 KEY CONTRIBUTIONS POLITICAL PHILOSOPHY, ETHICS

CLASSICAL LIBERALISM

Classical liberalism emphasized **civil liberties**, often **advocated democracy** or some form of **social contract theory**, and the **economic free market**. Most liberals favoured **minimal state involvement** in **politics**, **ethics**, and **economics**, which were seen as **complementary attitudes**: **freedom of speech and belief** went hand in hand with the **freedom to pursue one's own business interests**. This led to the **birth of capitalism**.

DIVISION OF LABOUR

Smith argued that **economic wealth grows through a number of factors**, but primarily the ***division of labour***. It is simply **more efficient** for a **farmer** to **grow the wheat**, the **miller** to **grind it into flour**, and the **baker** to **turn it into bread**, than for a **single person to perform all tasks**. Greater efficiencies can be gained as tasks are **broken down further**, and the **competition** between the various **producers** and **providers of services** in this **chain** ensures that **costs** are **kept at a minimum**, **productivity increases**, and **wealth spreads through society** as the **labourers** in turn **spend their profits**.

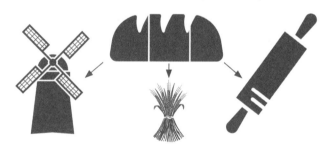

THE INVISIBLE HAND

Smith's key contribution was to propose that such **wealth creation** required **no centralized control**, but could be guided by the "**invisible hand**" of ***rational self-interest***. Better, then, to **leave the farmers**, **millers**, and **bakers alone**, and the **market to regulate itself**, for **competition** and **desire for profit** will **keep them from overcharging**. Of course, this **only works** if those **businesses pay their taxes**, **reinvest their profits at home**, and **do not form monopolies** or **enter secret price-fixing agreements**.

THE PHILOSOPHES

As a key figure in the Enlightenment, French philosopher Voltaire rejected the traditional notion of God in favour of an impersonal creator of the universe.

 NAME VOLTAIRE (FRANÇOIS-MARIE AROUET)

 DATES 1694–1778

 NATIONALITY FRENCH

 SCHOOL PHILOSOPHES

 MAIN WORKS *PHILOSOPHICAL LETTERS; CANDIDE*

KEY CONTRIBUTIONS PHILOSOPHY OF RELIGION

DEISM

Voltaire was a noted ***philosophe***, or **public intellectual**, whose ideas influenced the **precepts** behind the **French Revolution**. A **keen critic of the Church**, Voltaire favoured a **doctrine** that has since become known as ***deism***. Other **notable deists** included **Thomas Jefferson** and **Thomas Paine**, and it's an idea that has influenced **Freemasonry** and the **Unitarian** faith.

NATURAL THEOLOGY

The **basic premise of deism** is that, while deists agree that the **universe** was created by a deity, this is **not the personal God** of the **orthodox religions** who **speaks to believers directly** or **via revelation**. It is a more **distant** and **impersonal force** that can **only be understood indirectly** by the **application of reason**. This approach to **understanding God** is known as ***natural theology***.

CANDIDE

We can therefore understand God by looking at **nature**. An example of this would be the design argument (considered elsewhere), which traces the **hand of the creator** in the **natural world**. However, **Voltaire** argued, we **should resist seeing the events of the natural world** in ***moral*** terms. He famously satirized this approach in his novel ***Candide***, which is primarily aimed at the philosopher **Leibniz**, who argued that we live in the **best of all possible worlds**. Faced as we are with **war**, **torture**, **famine**, **flood**, **earthquake**, and other causes of **natural** and **manmade suffering**, it **strains reason** to consider such events as happening "for the best".

TRANSCENDENTAL IDEALISM

While sharing empiricism's view that we can have no direct knowledge of a world beyond experience, Immanuel Kant argued that we can, however, understand how the mind itself sets the limits of knowledge.

 NAME IMMANUEL KANT

 DATES 1724–1804

 NATIONALITY GERMAN

 SCHOOL KANTIAN IDEALISM

 MAIN WORKS *CRITIQUE OF PURE REASON; PROLEGOMENA TO ANY FUTURE METAPHYSICS; GROUNDWORK OF THE METAPHYSIC OF MORALS; CRITIQUE OF PRACTICAL REASON; CRITIQUE OF JUDGMENT*

 KEY CONTRIBUTIONS ETHICS, METAPHYSICS, EPISTEMOLOGY, AESTHETICS, PHILOSOPHY OF RELIGION

THE PROBLEM OF SCEPTICISM

Rationalists such as **Leibniz** and **Descartes** believed that there were **innate ideas** or **principles** that acted as **guarantees** of **certain types of knowledge**. It was **Hume**, among others, who convinced **Kant** that such ideas **could not be discovered** purely by **reason** *or* **experience**. What, then, can **guarantee the truth of sense experience**?

PHENOMENA AND NOUMENA

Kant advances a form of *idealism*: in his terms, we **only ever have access to sense experience** (the *phenomenon*), and **not to the world of objects** that *transcends* and lies behind such experience (the *noumenon*). As a result, the **transcendental reality** – the *noumenal* **world** – while it **may exist**, will **always remain hidden from us**.

CATEGORIES OF THE UNDERSTANDING

However, Kant's insight was to see that we could **still learn** about the **nature of the world** via the way in which our **understanding** *shapes* experience. We know that "**every effect has a cause**", that **space** and **time** have a **certain structure**, that **matter exists**, etc., because without such **built-in assumptions** (*categories of the understanding*), our **experiences would be incomprehensible**. In other words, somewhat like a TV that **translates electrical signals into pictures**, our **minds** *impose* **causation**, **space**, **time**, **matter**, and so forth on **raw experiences** *in order to* **make sense of them**. Therefore, **time** and **space**, etc., **do not exist in themselves**, but are the **forms** that **our understanding takes**.

DEONTOLOGY

The deontological approach to ethics proposes that good actions must obey the moral law, an approach best exemplified by Kant.

THE GOOD WILL

You might **act** out of **pity**, out of **friendship**, or just because it **makes you feel good**, but for **Kant** the **only reason** to do the **right thing** is out of **duty** to the **moral law**. It is therefore **only this motivation** – what Kant termed the **Good Will** – that **makes an action moral**.

moral action

friendship

pity

duty

THE CATEGORICAL IMPERATIVE

But **how do we know what the moral law is?** If you want to **get fit**, you **must** take up some form of **exercise**. This is a **hypothetical imperative** – something you must do **only if** you want to get fit. In contrast, "**do not steal**" is a **categorical imperative**; it is something **you *must*** do **in all circumstances, regardless of personal inclination**.

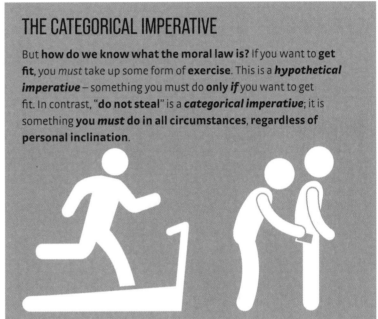

CONTRADICTION IN CONCEPTION

To be a moral law a principle must be **universal**, and the way to **test this** is to see if **not obeying it would lead to a contradiction**. This can happen in **two ways**. If it's fine to **steal**, then there **would be no such thing as a right to property** – the very **concept** of "**mine**" and "**yours**" would **disappear**, for **no one could complain** if things were **taken** from them. **Universalising "it's fine to steal"** therefore results in a **contradiction in conception** (a **contradiction in the very idea itself**).

CONTRADICTION IN WILL

But **not every immoral act is self-contradictory** in this way. **Some obligations** are merely what Kant termed **imperfect duties**. We **all need help** to get by in life, so we should really **help others**, but it's **not logically self-contradictory to believe** that "**no one should help one another**", for it's **possible to imagine such a society**. However, my believing this would certainly **undermine achieving my goals**, and is therefore what Kant calls a **contradiction in will** (**willing something** that is **against my own intentions**).

RIGHTS

Kant's moral philosophy also supplies a deontological basis for human rights, a principle that is known as his Formula of Humanity.

FORMULA OF HUMANITY

Kant's **categorical imperative** also implies that we **should not use other people as a means to our own ends**, but should treat them as **ends in themselves**. This basically means that you **shouldn't use** or **coerce people**, **trick them** into doing something, or otherwise **stop them from following their own legitimate goals** in life.

MEANS AND ENDS

If I **sell someone a painting** I know is **forged**, I thereby **rob them** of their **right to be dealt with honestly**, and to **know the truth**. They have a **legitimate desire** to **own a genuine thing of beauty**, and I've supplied them with a **fake** painting just to **make money**. I'm therefore **using them** (their own **honesty** and **trusting nature**) as a **means to my own ends** (**money**).

NATURAL RIGHTS

While Kant's approach may be used to argue that **human rights** are **tied to a person's possession of reason**, other philosophers have tried to base them in the idea of the **social contract**. For instance, **Hobbes and Locke** believed that citizens possessed "**natural rights**" to **property**, **safety**, **freedom**, etc., which, in return for **obedience**, the state was **morally bound to enforce**.

UTILITARIANISM

However, **utilitarianism** would seem to present a **problem for the notion of rights**. Bentham **dismissed** the idea of **natural rights**, arguing that **rights can only be granted by legal convention**, and that even this is **subject to utilitarian calculations**. In a modern thought experiment – known as the "**ticking time bomb scenario**" – **torturing a terrorist suspect** regarding an **impending attack** may **violate their human** right forbidding "**cruel and unusual punishment**", but is this **outweighed by the lives at stake**? Bentham would say that it is.

THE SUBLIME

In aesthetics, a beautiful work of art may produce feelings of pleasure and admiration, whereas a sublime thing may inspire feelings of awe, fear, and even horror.

PLEASURE

While philosophers such as **Plato** and **Aristotle** saw **beauty** as related to **pleasure**, later philosophers – such as **Edmund Burke**, **Kant**, and **Schopenhauer** – argued that certain **aesthetic experiences** represent a **distinct category**. For while we may admire a **beautiful painting** for its **intricate detail**, **harmony of form**, or **graceful composition**, the **grandeur** and **vastness** of a **mountain range** seems to go **beyond pleasure** into something **less easily definable**.

You

BOUNDLESSNESS

The **difference** between the two **experiences has** been **analysed in different ways**, but the **key distinction** would seem to be that **sublime things unsettle us**. While giving us **pleasure**, a **view** of the **Grand Canyon** or the **Himalayas** may also make us feel **insignificant** or even **afraid**. As Kant argued, we are **overwhelmed** by the subject's ***boundlessness*** – our **mind** is **boggled** by its **vastness**, or its **extreme age** – such as when we **compare human life** to the **size** and **age** of the **universe**.

THE NUMINOUS

The notion of the **sublime** also has **religious connotations**. In ***The Idea of the Holy***, German theologian **Rudolf Otto** (1869–1937) proposed that certain **mysterious qualities of God** are ***numinous*** – they are both **terrifying** and **fascinating**. This **ambivalence** is perhaps best brought out through consideration of the concept of "**awe**". If a thing is "**awful**", in the modern sense, then it is **bad** or **terrible**, but a thing that is "**awesome**" fills us with **wonder**. When we say that **God's numinous qualities** – such as his **power** and **vastness** – fill us with "awe", we therefore mean that we **feel** both **terror** and **wonder**.

THE ARGUMENT FROM MORALITY

The argument from morality attempts to prove the existence of God by claiming that in order for morality to exist there must be an independent source of moral goodness.

CONSCIENCE

Perhaps the **simplest form of this argument** is that **human beings seem to possess a moral conscience**. Since this often **advises against self-gratification** and **other forms of self-interest**, we may wonder where this "**inner voice**" comes from. However, of course, such a "voice" **need not be divine**, for – as **Freud** argued in his notion of the *superego* – we may simply **internalize** the **values** and **opinions** of **social elders**, **parents**, and **teachers**.

MORAL GOODNESS

Another variation of this approach proposes that **unless ethical standards have an independent source**, then **all moral values** are in fact **relative**. Therefore, **either God exists** or there can be **no such thing as morality**. Of course, this **only applies if we accept some form of *moral realism***, which assumes that **moral values must be fixed** and **objective**. However, **opponents argue that this is not the case**: a cursory survey reveals that there are indeed **significant differences between what is considered "good" in different cultures and across time**, suggesting that **morality** is, to a certain extent at least, **relative**.

JUST DESERTS

One of the most interesting forms of this argument is supplied by **Kant**. We are entitled to think that **being moral leads to happiness** – otherwise, **why be moral in the first place?** However, **doing the right thing might not always be easy or pleasant**, and **people who act morally frequently don't get what they deserve**. The **only way acting morally can be justified** is if this **apparent *injustice*** is **rectified in the afterlife**, where **good people get their rewards**.

CONSERVATISM

A founder of modern conservatism, Edmund Burke argued that a stable and just society requires respect for institutions and traditional values.

 NAME EDMUND BURKE

 DATES 1729–97

 NATIONALITY IRISH

 SCHOOL CONSERVATISM

 MAIN WORKS *A VINDICATION OF NATURAL SOCIETY; ON THE SUBLIME AND BEAUTIFUL; REFLECTIONS ON THE REVOLUTION IN FRANCE*

 KEY CONTRIBUTIONS POLITICAL PHILOSOPHY, AESTHETICS

OLD WHIGS

As a member of the **Whig Party**, **Burke** had many **liberal sympathies**, including concern for **curbing royal power**, **protecting Catholics against persecution**, and **support for the grievances of American colonists** in their **tax dispute with Great Britain** (which would eventually spark the **American War of Independence**). However, the events of the **French Revolution** of 1789 **divided the Whig Party**, with Burke and other "**Old Whigs**" turning against the "**New Whigs**" who **supported its progressive and rationalist ideals**.

JACOBINISM

In ***Reflections on the Revolution in France***, Burke outlined what he saw as the **problems with French Jacobinism**, the **revolutionary political movement** seeking to **reshape France** via **radical liberal ideals**. While Jacobins drew on the **rationalist philosophies** of **Rousseau** and **Voltaire**, basing **political liberty** on **each individual's inalienable possession of abstract *rights***, Burke argued that such an approach would **not guarantee social order**. So, even before the **worst excesses** of the ***Reign of Terror***, which decimated Parisian society with **executions**, **imprisonment**, and **persecution**, Burke **forewarned** that such **root-and-branch reformation** would only cause **disaster**.

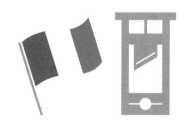

PREJUDICE

Instead, Burke argued that a society's **rights** and **moral values** were preserved in its **institutions** and **traditions**, **religious organizations**, **nobility**, **laws** and **customs**, **armed forces**, and its **commercial** and **manufacturing activities**. As such, a nation is **not just a serious set of rationally decided principles**, but the accumulation of centuries of human wisdom and best practice, which develops in us what Burke called "**prejudice**", or the **almost instinctual reverence for what is good**.

REVOLUTION

English-born revolutionary philosopher Thomas Paine argued that a nation's people had a right to overthrow its own government if its actions contravened fundamental natural rights.

 NAME THOMAS PAINE

 DATES 1737–1809

 NATIONALITY ENGLISH-BORN AMERICAN

 SCHOOL LIBERALISM

 MAIN WORKS *COMMON SENSE; RIGHTS OF MAN; THE AGE OF REASON*

 KEY CONTRIBUTIONS POLITICAL PHILOSOPHY

SEDITION

In his *Rights of Man* (1791), **Paine defended** the **ideals of the French Revolution against Edmund Burke's conservative attack**, building upon earlier ideas set out in *Common Sense* (1776) and other writings that had played a **key role in American independence**. For this, he was **tried** and **convicted** of **seditious libel** in his own absence (being then in France), ensuring that he could **never again return to England**.

COMMON SENSE

Paine's main target is **hereditary monarchy** and **privilege**, which he saw as fostering **corruption**, **inequality**, and **tyranny**. In contrast, he envisaged a **democratic republic** whose **constitution protected the pre-existing natural human rights of each individual**, where the **right to vote** was **universal** and **not based on property ownership**, and that acknowledged **each person's inherent capacity** (their *common sense*) to **perceive truth**, and therefore **did not require** the **guidance of kings or priests**. As such, Paine is often described as a *deist* (like **Voltaire**), believing in a **supreme creator deity** that – unlike the God of Christianity – did not communicate through revelation or intervene in human affairs.

REFORM

And yet, despite **advancing the causes of Britain's enemies** – it was even said that he discussed with **Napoleon** methods for **invading England** – Paine was still **primarily concerned with reforming his homeland**. Among the **suggested reforms** set out in *Rights of Man* are the **abolition of hereditary titles**, the **establishment of an American-style constitution**, **progressive taxation** based on **level of income** and **ability to pay**, and various **social** and **educational programmes**.

UTILITARIANISM

Rather than view moral questions traditionally, in relation to abstract concepts of "good" or "bad", Jeremy Bentham redefined them in natural terms, involving the happiness of the greatest number.

 NAME JEREMY BENTHAM

 DATES 1748–1832

 NATIONALITY ENGLISH

 SCHOOL UTILITARIAN

 MAIN WORKS *INTRODUCTION TO THE PRINCIPLES OF MORALS AND LEGISLATION; THE RATIONALE OF PUNISHMENT*

 KEY CONTRIBUTIONS ETHICS, POLITICAL PHILOSOPHY

THE PRINCIPLE OF UTILITY

Whereas **Plato** saw **good acts** as those that embodied the **pure idea** of "the Good", and **Kant** saw them in terms of **rational duty**, **Bentham** equated "**good**" with **pleasure**, and the **"right" action** as that which has the greatest *utility* (**usefulness**) in bringing about the **most pleasure** while incurring the **least pain**.

CRIME AND PUNISHMENT

For instance, in **opposing the death penalty**, Bentham argued that **all punishment has three aims: protecting society**, **reforming criminals**, and **deterring potential wrongdoers**. And yet, there are **more effective ways** of serving these aims than **taking the criminal's life**, and it's therefore questionable whether the **pain of the convict's death**, the **grief of his family**, the **loss of good that a reformed criminal might do**, etc., is actually **outweighed by the benefits of his death**. Judged purely on its **consequences**, then, **capital punishment should be abolished**.

QUANTIFYING HAPPINESS

However, if we judge the **morality of an action** on its **consequences**, such a **calculation** will probably prove **very complicated**. To aid in such decisions, Bentham evolved something he called the **Felicific Calculus**, which set out **various criteria** that each **potential action** should be **judged by**. In doing so, Bentham **simplifies ethical dilemmas** by attempting to **quantify "happiness"**.

THE FELICIFIC CALCULUS

Intensity: How much pleasure?
Duration: How long will it last?
Likelihood: How likely is it?
Remoteness: How soon will it happen?
Frequency: How often will it occur?
Purity: How pure is the experience?
Scope: How many will feel it?

Compare **taking heroin** with **reading a book**. Drugged ecstasy may be **intense**, but **short-lasting**, and it's **easier to visit the library** than score **illegal drugs**, which also **risks imprisonment**. Plus, there's the **unpleasant withdrawal symptoms**, the **detriment to health**, **bank balance**, and **capacity to function in society**. Enjoyable books, by contrast, are **plentiful**, and reading is an activity that makes you **more educated**, a **better conversationalist**, and an **overall benefit to society**. Reading wins!

ANIMAL RIGHTS

Before Bentham, philosophers had failed to recognize the moral status of animals, but utilitarianism opened up a new perspective that put humans and creatures on the same level.

MORAL AGENTS

Descartes had notoriously **dismissed** the **suffering of animals** as the **unconscious behaviour of biological machines**. Even **Kant** considered that we only have an **indirect duty not to harm them unnecessarily**, because it **reflects badly on us**: being cruel to animals sets a **bad example**, and breeds **bad moral habits**.

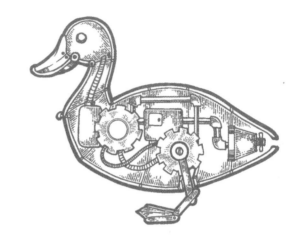

SLAVERY

In contrast, by **framing morality in natural terms**, the question of whether or not our **treatment of animals** was moral came down to **whether it caused them suffering**. Bentham saw that at the heart of the **mistreatment** of animals was the **common assumption that they did not possess reason**, and could **not converse**. But, he argued, if that is the basis for being considered a **moral agent**, many humans – **infants, adults with certain mental disabilities** – don't qualify. In fact, he saw in this assumption the supposed **justification for slavery** and the **racist exploitation** of **"inferior" non-White cultures**. Rather than invoke **reason** and **language**, Bentham therefore argued that it is only *sentience* (the **ability to feel pain or pleasure**) that should matter.

RIGHTS

This said, Bentham **did not think animals possessed "rights"** as such – but nor, for that matter, did he think **humans** did either. The only issue was **suffering**. Since an animal (arguably) does not know it will die, then **as long as it is happy when it is alive**, or else its **sufferings are outweighed by the consequent benefits to society in general**, its **use for food or medical research** was **permissible**.

WOMEN'S RIGHTS

Throughout much of history and across cultures, women have played a secondary role to men, a situation that has only begun to change in relatively recent times.

FIRST-WAVE FEMINISM

The **history of feminism** is often divided into **three "waves"**, the **first liberal form** focusing on **providing women** with the **basic rights so far denied them** – such as **property ownership**, the **right to vote**, and **even to enter certain professions**. This process would take some time, and in **some countries** is **still ongoing**, the **UK first allowing certain women to vote in local elections in 1859**, but **not granting full suffrage until 1928**, by which time it had **already spread through most Western countries**.

 NAME MARY WOLLSTONECRAFT

 **DATES** 1759–97

 NATIONALITY ENGLISH

 SCHOOL ENLIGHTENMENT PHILOSOPHY

MAIN WORKS *A VINDICATION OF THE RIGHTS OF WOMAN*

KEY CONTRIBUTIONS POLITICAL PHILOSOPHY, ETHICS

The **First Wave** or Liberal Feminism – nineteenth/early twentieth century – property, voting, and other legal rights

Second Wave or Radical Feminism – 1960s/70s – equal pay, reproductive rights, career opportunities

Third Wave – 1990s onward – questioning notions of binary sex and sexuality, race, gender and womanhood

REVOLUTION

In light of this, **Mary Wollstonecraft – philosopher, novelist, revolutionary** – was **far ahead of the curve**, her *Vindication of the Rights of Woman* laying the **foundation for later developments in sexual equality**. Inspired by the **republican ideals** that drove the **French Revolution** – even **travelling to France** to **aid** in the **revolutionary struggle** – she nonetheless saw that *liberté* and *egalité* did not **always extend to women**.

EDUCATION

A central target of *A Vindication* is French philosopher **Rousseau** (discussed earlier), whose *Émile* pictured the **ideal education** for its **titular protagonist**, designed to develop both **reason** and **emotion**, while **simultaneously denying Sophie** (his **future wife**) the **same curriculum**. In Rousseau's view, the **primary purpose of female education** was to **equip women for being man's** *companion* (and the **domestic duties** that entailed). But, arguing that we are **all made in God's image**, Wollstonecraft took issue with this **sexist bias**: given the **same education** and **opportunities**, there was **no reason woman should or could not be** the **equal of man**.

THE DIALECTIC

Hegel argued that human society does not progress along a straight and rising line, but advances in a gradual zig-zag through opposing values and ideas towards an ultimate goal.

 NAME GEORGE WILHELM FRIEDRICH HEGEL

 DATES 1770–1831

 NATIONALITY GERMAN

 SCHOOL GERMAN IDEALISM

 MAIN WORKS *THE PHENOMENOLOGY OF SPIRIT; THE SCIENCE OF LOGIC; THE PHILOSOPHY OF HISTORY*

 KEY CONTRIBUTIONS METAPHYSICS, EPISTEMOLOGY, POLITICAL PHILOSOPHY, LOGIC

PHILOSOPHICAL OPPOSITION

Dialectic is simply a form of **philosophical argument** involving **opposing positions**: a *thesis*, and its *antithesis*. If this argument reaches a **deeper understanding**, then a new, **third position** is produced: a *synthesis*.

Thesis: Sweet things are bad for you

Antithesis: Sweet things are nice

Synthesis: Sweet things are fine in moderation

Thesis: Disciplined society

Antithesis: Liberal society

Synthesis: Moderate society

HISTORICAL PROGRESSION

Hegel uses this form of argument to suggest that **each stage of history** is an attempt to **balance out previous extremes**, as **each contains an element of truth**. A society is overly **strict** and **disciplinarian**; the **next generation rebels**, producing a **fun-living society** focused on **freedom** and **pleasure**; a **third generation**, sated by **meaningless excess** and **rootless freedom**, **moderates its behaviour** and **resurrects milder versions of former traditions**.

POLITICAL EVOLUTION

Despite its **religious connotations**, this notion of **inevitable progress** and **self-realization** has also inspired **atheist and secular philosophers**. **Karl Marx** pictured the **ideal communist state** as the **Hegelian synthesis** of **feudalism** and **capitalism**. **Francis Fukuyama**, in his ***End of History and the Last Man***, saw in the **fall of the Berlin Wall** an **end to** the **competing ideologies** of **communism** and **capitalism**, and therefore of **history itself**. However, as subsequent events have suggested, **either Hegel was wrong**, or **history isn't finished yet**.

THE ABSOLUTE

For Hegel, this dialectic process **leads to a final goal**. As the **human spirit** that drives history **evolves**, the **opposites** that it **expresses itself through** become more **refined** and **inclusive**, until finally **everything is united** in a **single**, almost **mystical** moment of **self-awareness**, which Hegel termed *the **Absolute***.

PESSIMISM

Arthur Schopenhauer argued that Nature expressed a blind will fundamentally at odds with human reason, a conflict that made existence a constant source of suffering.

 NAME ARTHUR SCHOPENHAUER

 DATES 1788–1860

 NATIONALITY GERMAN

 SCHOOL TRANSCENDENTAL IDEALISM/PESSIMISM

 MAIN WORKS *THE WORLD AS WILL AND REPRESENTATION*

 KEY CONTRIBUTIONS ETHICS, METAPHYSICS, AESTHETICS

WILL AND REPRESENTATION

Drawing on the work of **Kant**, **Schopenhauer** divided reality into **will** and **representation**. But while he agreed with Kant that **perception** (*representation*) was a sort of **mental veil thrown over the world**, he argued that what Kant called the **thing-in-itself** – the **reality behind appearances** that we can **never directly perceive** – was actually **felt in us** through the **natural forces** that **express themselves** in **instinct** and **desire** (the *will*). In a sense, then, our **motives** are the **expression** of that **unperceivable reality**.

HIDDEN INFLUENCES

For Schopenhauer, **God did not exist**, and **Nature** was **indifferent to human concerns**. It is for this reason that he is considered a ***philosophical pessimist***. *Will* does not care about human beings, or the **rational order** and **moral values** that we **try to impose upon affairs**, but **aims rather at its own natural ends**. Thus, as **Darwin** and **Freud** would later argue, often unconscious animal instincts are forever **influencing** and **undermining** our **conscious purposes**. This is the **source of all misery**.

ASCETICISM

What, then, was the answer? **Social progress** was **futile**, for **humans will always be driven by Will**. For **Schopenhauer**, as for **Buddhism** (which he **later discovered** with approval), the **only solution** was to **turn our back on desire** and try to **escape into a world of pure**, **ascetic contemplation**, where we might **lose our sense of self** and all its attendant desires, **pains**, and **pleasures**.

ANTHROPOMORPHISM

Feuerbach argued that religion filled a human need, and that God was essentially a projection of human qualities.

 NAME LUDWIG FEUERBACH

 DATES 1804–72

 NATIONALITY GERMAN

 SCHOOL HUMANISM

 MAIN WORKS *THE ESSENCE OF CHRISTIANITY*

 KEY CONTRIBUTIONS PHILOSOPHY OF RELIGION

HUMANISM

While not completely **unsympathetic to aspects of religion** (he **denied being "atheist"** in the accepted sense of the time), **Feuerbach** attempted to understand the **concept of God** in **human**, as opposed to **theological or mystical, terms**. As such, his approach is a form of ***humanism***, and his account of **God as human projection** would **influence thinkers such as Marx, Freud**, and **Nietzsche**.

PROJECTION

Since we **cannot understand an infinite being**, we **necessarily project upon it** our **own human values**, but **greatly magnified**. God is **omniscient** (**all-knowing**), an **expansion of human intelligence**. He is **omnipotent** (all-powerful), an **amplification of human strength**. His **compassion** is simply **human love writ large**.

RELIGIOUS LANGUAGE

Feuerbach's notion of **religious projection** actually stems from an **old theological debate** about whether in fact we can **speak meaningfully about God**.

← "positive way"   "negative way" →

POSITIVE AND NEGATIVE

Proponents of ***cataphatic theology*** argue that there is **some connection between divine and human qualities** – between **God's** and **humanity's wisdom, strength**, etc. But those who **deny this** advocate a ***via negativa*** or ***negative way*** (***apophatic theology***), arguing that **God is so different from us** that we **can only speak about him in terms of what he is *not***. Feuerbach uses this limitation to imply not just that the **positive approach is mistaken**, but that God (as **traditionally conceived**) is ***merely* a projection of human qualities**. But it can be seen here that the debate need not be one of **belief versus atheism**, but can also be taken as a controversy about the **nature of religious language**.

 small   cruel   weak   unforgiving

ETHICAL EGOISM

Whereas Marx used Hegel's philosophy to argue that society must evolve toward communal obligations, Max Stirner argued that the only duty a person has is to his own self.

 NAME MAX STIRNER

 DATES 1806–56

 NATIONALITY GERMAN

 SCHOOL EGOISM/INDIVIDUALIST ANARCHISM

 MAIN WORKS *THE EGO AND ITS OWN*

 KEY CONTRIBUTIONS ETHICS

INDIVIDUALISM

Stirner is an interesting figure. He is often claimed as an **anarchist**, but unlike **Kropotkin** or **Bakunin**, he **rejected** any form of **social organization**. In other ways, he foreshadows existentialism, believing that we must be **authentic to ourselves**. To do this, he believed we must **withdraw our allegiance** from **false concepts** and **ideologies imposed from outside** – whether **religious**, **political**, or **philosophical**. He is therefore perhaps best thought of as an *individualist*.

VOLUNTARY EGOISM

Stirner argued that those who **think they act out** of "altruism" or "goodness" (*involuntary egoists*) **fool themselves**, for we are actually **all driven** to seek our own **self-interest**. We must therefore **embrace this fact** (become *voluntary egoists*). In this advice Stirner distinguishes himself from *psychological egoists* such as **Freud**, who thought we should **resist**, **sublimate**, and transcend our **selfish drives**, and aligns himself with *ethical egoists* such as **Nietzsche**, who argued that following our *will to power* was actually **a road to happiness** and **fulfilment**.

PROPERTY AND OWNERSHIP

For Stirner, the **self** has **no essence** or **character**, and no inherent "**rationality**" that can act as the **basis** for **ethical** or **communal standards**. How, then, are **property** and **rights protected**? In **ethical** and **legal** terms, they aren't. That **belongs to you** only which it is **in your own power** to **acquire** and **retain**. There may possibly exist **loose affiliations** of **voluntary egoists**, Stirner proposes, but such a "**society**" seems potentially quite **brutal**, and it's difficult to see **how it could persist**.

RULE UTILITARIANISM

While John Stuart Mill broadly agreed with the principles behind Bentham's utilitarianism, he thought that simple pleasure was too crude a standard with which to equate goodness.

 NAME JOHN STUART MILL

 DATES 1806–73

 NATIONALITY ENGLISH

 SCHOOL UTILITARIANISM

 MAIN WORKS *ON LIBERTY; UTILITARIANISM; ON REPRESENTATIVE GOVERNMENT*

 KEY CONTRIBUTIONS ETHICS, POLITICAL PHILOSOPHY

THE QUALITY OF PLEASURE

For **Bentham**, there were **no distinctions** in the **quality of pleasure**. A **pleasurable act** might come **admixed with pain** or other **unpleasant consequences**, but **whatever the act in question**, the **pleasure involved** was **always of the same sort**. Whether **poetry** or **pub games**, the only question that **distinguished actions** was the *amount* of **pleasure** (or **pain**) they produced.

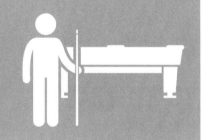

SOCRATES AND THE PIG

But **Mill** thought this **wrong**: it is much **better**, he said, even to be an **unhappy human being** than a **happy animal**; better to be **Socrates** *dissatisfied* than a *satisfied* pig. The **quality of pleasure** counted for something, and an **intellectual life struggling with eternal questions** was to be **preferred** to the **unexamined life of simple hedonism**.

ACT UTILITARIANISM

As well as **disagreeing** on the **quality of pleasure**, **Mill** pointed out that **Bentham's utilitarianism** was **limited to single acts**. But whether a particular action brings **more pleasure** is something that may **change** according to **fluctuating factors**. And – Bentham's **Felicific Calculus** aside – it's also something that's **difficult to calculate**. But most of all, **act utilitarianism** seems to **justify** what we traditionally would consider **immoral acts**: if, on a particular occasion, **framing an innocent person** for a crime makes **judges**, **jury**, and **press** **happy** that they've **found the culprit**, then **should it be favoured**? To combat this, Mill proposed instead that we follow *rules of conduct* that – in general – lead to the **best results**. And, overall, a consistently **corrupt justice system doesn't benefit society as a whole**.

THE PRINCIPLE OF HARM

Mill was a philosophical liberal who argued that society should only regulate those actions that harm others or restrict their freedom.

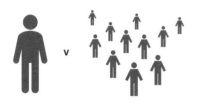

THE TYRANNY OF THE MAJORITY

The **problem with utilitarianism** – and with **democracy in general** – is that there is a **potential** for what **Mill** termed *the **tyranny of the majority***. Because even a **well-governed society** will reflect the **values** and **ideas** of the **majority of its members**, those who **do not share** these are liable to be **marginalized** or **persecuted**.

SELF-REGARDING ACTIONS

To protect **individual freedom**, **Mill** therefore argued that **society's laws** should **only relate** to those **actions that affect others**. If I **steal** from you or **threaten** you with **violence**, I **infringe on your rights to legal ownership and personal safety** respectively. So, **society** should **step in** to **stop such harms**. All else – what Mill termed ***self-regarding*** actions – should be **left alone**. Though I am **free to express my displeasure** at your **taste in music** or your **unhealthy eating habits**, I have **no right to force you** to abandon such things.

FREEDOM OF SPEECH

Mill's **principle of harm** is therefore a sort of **golden rule** for both **personal conduct** and **public legislation**. It also sets a **limit** to what **can and can't be said**. Mostly, Mill is against **censorship**, arguing that **repressed views** rob us of **correct minority opinions** that might **challenge** the **false views** of the **majority** (just think of how **votes for women** and the **abolition of slavery** were all once minority views). Censorship also **encourages dissenters to hide views** that **public discussion** might **correct** in a way that is **beneficial to all**. The only **limit to speech** is where it passes over into **incitement** – that is, where **words encourage physical harm**, such as a call for someone to be **physically attacked**.

DEMOCRACY

Mill argued that modern democracy must take the form of representative government, where the vote is extended to all literate adults.

IDEAL DEMOCRACY

Although it **failed to meet** the **democratic ideal** in other ways (its use of **slaves**, its attitude to **women** and **immigrants**), the **democracy of ancient Athens** is often viewed with nostalgia as the **last point at which "true" democracy existed**. This is because it allowed **many individuals** a *direct* **say in political affairs** – something that **modern democracies**, where **voters elect** a *representative* to speak for them, **cannot do on logistical grounds**.

Ideal

v

Representative

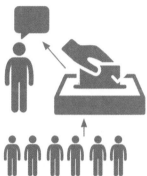

PARTICIPATION

Mill accepts this, arguing that **representative democracy** is the **best form of government** and **superior** to a **benign dictatorship**. However, he also argues that **modern democracies fall short** of the **democratic ideal** on other counts. During the latter half of the nineteenth century **most existing democracies still excluded women** and the **poor** from **voting**. But, Mill argued, **wealth was irrelevant**, and **intellectual** and **moral differences** between **men** and **women**, or **people in general**, mainly stem from **upbringing**. By **extending participation** and **educating** the **voting populace**, though, we encourage people to become **fuller citizens in matters in which they have a say**, which – on **utilitarian grounds** – **can only make a society happier**.

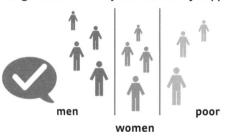

men

women

poor

OPINION

But Mill also recognized **dangers in extending voting entitlement**. A person's **knowledge** of **ethics** and **politics** comes largely through **opinion** and **experience**, so it's vital that the **populace** is **educated** in the **skills required to analyse issues**. So, as well as educating voters, we need to **safeguard** against the *tyranny of the majority* (discussed earlier) by **preserving expertise**. Mill therefore proposed that **more educated individuals should be allotted more votes**, and that an ideal parliament should consist of two chambers, the second consisting **of intellectually eminent people** that would **oversee the actions** of the first.

EVOLUTION

Although of primary importance as a scientific theory, the theory of evolution has a number of important philosophical consequences.

 NAME CHARLES DARWIN

 DATES 1809–82

 NATIONALITY ENGLISH

 SCHOOL EVOLUTIONARY BIOLOGY

 MAIN WORKS *THE VOYAGE OF THE BEAGLE; THE ORIGIN OF SPECIES; THE DESCENT OF MAN*

 KEY CONTRIBUTIONS METAPHYSICS

HUMANS AND ANIMALS

Jointly proposed by naturalists **Charles Darwin** and **Alfred Russel Wallace** (1823–1913), though now most commonly associated with Darwin alone, the **theory of evolution by natural selection** provides an **alternative to supernatural accounts** of the **origin** and **development** of **life on Earth**. Rather than humans being **God-ordained rulers of the world**, or the **possessors of unique intellectual or moral capacities**, evolution proposes that we are essentially **no different from animals**, from which we are in fact **descended**.

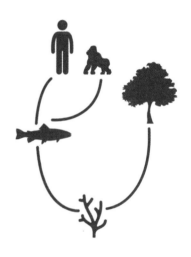

NATURAL SELECTION

The driving force of evolution is ***natural selection***. As **modern genetics** has revealed, **organisms pass natural traits** to **descendants** through **genes**. **Tall parents** tend to have **tall children**. However, sometimes the **height gene** of a **smaller ancestor** still carried (***latent***) in a **parent's DNA** can be **passed on instead**. Also, **Nature** occasionally makes **mistakes** in the **gene-copying process**, and ***mutations*** occur, resulting in **unexpected variations**. The **environment** in which an organism finds itself then helps ***naturally select*** which organisms **survive** to **reproduce** and **pass on their genes**. Over the slow march of **millennia**, this relatively simple process has produced the **myriad species** that inhabit Earth.

SOCIAL DARWINISM

Philosophically, evolution is interesting because it proposes that **Nature is not *teleological*** (has **no purpose** or **goal**) – the planet's **dominant species** might have evolved from **lizards** or **dolphins**, rather than **apes**. But there is also its **consequence for ethics**: if – some argue – humans have evolved through **power** and **dominance**, the **strong** and "**well adapted**" surviving at the **expense of the weak**, shouldn't **morality** and **society reflect this**? (Er…no!)

ANGST

Søren Kierkegaard argued that the price humans pay for their freedom is a deep-seated anxiety regarding just how they should use it.

NAME SØREN KIERKEGAARD

DATES 1813–55

NATIONALITY DANISH

SCHOOL EXISTENTIALISM

MAIN WORKS *THE CONCEPT OF ANXIETY; EITHER/OR; FEAR AND TREMBLING; THE SICKNESS UNTO DEATH*

KEY CONTRIBUTIONS ETHICS, PHILOSOPHY OF RELIGION

EXISTENTIAL DREAD

Unlike the **specific fear** we might feel in relation to a **present danger** – an **onrushing car**, facing a **wild bear** – or a more **low-level concern** – coping with the **rent**, a visit to the **dentist** – **angst** (also sometimes *anxiety*) is a more **generalized feeling**. While it **may be revealed** in **specific situations**, it is rather a **consequence of human existence** – which is why it is sometimes referred to as *existential dread*.

SELF-DESTRUCTIVE URGES

Standing on top of a **high building**, you may **imagine throwing yourself off**; driving a **car**, you may **picture crashing into a wall**. Such **dark thoughts** are **not uncommon**, but rather than being **evidence** of some **self-destructive urge**, they are, Kierkegaard argues, a **consequence of our freedom**: we **can do anything**, should we **wish it** – and this is what **terrifies us**. It is a **constant low-level sense** of this that **underlies all our decisions**, and it is a feeling that we often try to **escape** or **drown out** with **pleasure** and **distraction**, only for it to **re-emerge** in **other ways**. There is **no escaping it**.

FAITH

What then is the **answer**? For Kierkegaard, it is **faith**. Like a **sailor** tossed on a **turbulent sea** who **looks up** at the **stars**, we must **fix our focus** on that which is **unchanging**, on the **eternal values** and **assurances** provided by **God**.

CIVIL DISOBEDIENCE

Henry David Thoreau argued that a citizen's duty was not to the law, but to his own conscience, and where the two conflicted, his only recourse was conscientious lawbreaking.

 NAME HENRY DAVID THOREAU

 DATES 1817–62

 NATIONALITY AMERICAN

 SCHOOL TRANSCENDENTALISM

 MAIN WORKS *CIVIL DISOBEDIENCE; WALDEN*

 KEY CONTRIBUTIONS ETHICS, POLITICAL PHILOSOPHY

TRANSCENDENTALISM

Thoreau was greatly influenced by *Transcendentalism*, a philosophical movement associated with **Ralph Waldo Emerson** (1803–82), among others, which preached **self-reliance** in **moral** and **spiritual** matters. It was this spirit of self-reliance that led Thoreau to undertake a **two-year experiment in simple living** at an isolated cabin near **Walden Pond**, Concord, Massachusetts (an experience detailed in *Walden*).

TAXATION

Here, Thoreau **refused a demand for unpaid taxes**, citing his **opposition** to the **American war with Mexico** and the **government's promotion of slavery**, resulting in his **imprisonment**. Although his **incarceration lasted a mere day** (unasked for, an **aunt paid his debts**), the incident illustrates **Thoreau's attitude to authority**: we should **act according to our conscience, regardless of the consequences**. If a **law** is **unjust**, **voting won't change it**, as the **system** is **set up** to make **law reform slow** and **impractical** – even the **Constitution**, in its original form, seemed to **allow slavery**.

LIMITED GOVERNMENT

But Thoreau is a complex figure. His **individualism** attracts **libertarians** and **anarchists**. **No government is ever completely justified**, and that "is **best which governs not at all**". However, he **did not oppose taxation for vital public services**, merely **those that support a government's corrupt political agenda**. While prepared to **peaceably face the consequences of his own lawbreaking**, he **wasn't a pacifist** – as can be seen in his **defence of abolitionist John Brown** (1800–59), who was **executed** for attempting to **provoke a slave revolt**. Combined with his **passionate environmentalism**, this would seem to make him a **likely advocate** for today's **Extinction Rebellion** movement, **protesting alongside those risking imprisonment for our planet's future**.

ALIENATION

Marx argued that an individual could never be happy or fulfilled in a capitalist society, as exploitation and inequality are built into the system itself.

 NAME KARL MARX

 DATES 1818–83

 NATIONALITY GERMAN

 SCHOOL MARXISM

 MAIN WORKS *CAPITAL; THE GERMAN IDEOLOGY; THE COMMUNIST MANIFESTO*

 KEY CONTRIBUTIONS POLITICAL PHILOSOPHY

THE LABOUR THEORY OF VALUE

Drawing on the work of **previous economists**, Marx adopted the *labour theory of value*. A product's **worth** reflected the **time and effort taken to produce it**. If a cabinet took a carpenter two weeks, that should be **reflected in its value**.

THE DIVISION OF LABOUR

But with **automation** and the **factory system**, capitalists **reduced** the cost and **time** involved in **production**. Through *division of labour*, where production could be **broken down into simple tasks**, a **production line** of **low-skilled** (and **low-paid**) **labourers** could **assemble products** in **far less time** than it took a **single skilled craftsman**, the **labour force** producing a **wide range** of goods that, **as individuals**, they had **no expertise in making**.

SUPPLY AND DEMAND

But **capitalism** sees **value** in terms of **supply and demand**. It doesn't matter **how long** the carpenter takes, but **how in-demand** the product is. An **abundance** of cabinets **forces the price down**, whereas a **shortage forces it up**. **Capitalists** therefore argued that it is the **market** that **should determine the price**, regardless of the **labour involved**.

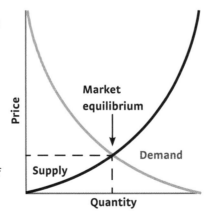

Price

Quantity

Market equilibrium

Demand

Supply

SURPLUS VALUE

This created *surplus value*. Paying labourers per hour (not completed task), plus time **saved** through automation, enabled greater production and **higher profits**. As such, instead of **farming** or **fishing** for their survival, workers became *alienated* from the product of their labour, paid to produce things they **didn't personally need** in order **to enrich someone else**.

SUPERSTRUCTURE

One of Marx's key insights was to show how capitalism shapes not just the relations between employers and workers, but the whole of culture and society.

CULTURAL REINFORCEMENT

Marx **divided society into two**: the **base** (or **substructure**) and the **superstructure**. "**Base**" described the **economic relations** between **employer** and **worker**, while **superstructure** described the **cultural productions** and **social relations** – such as **art** and **literature**, **religion** and **politics**, **family life**, **education**, and the **media**. However, not only does capitalism **determine the values that a society's culture expresses**, but these **cultural products** also **reinforce the economic relations that produced them**. Their **relationship** is **circular**.

"The cultural products and social forces that express and reinforce economic relations."

Superstructure

Base

"The economic relations between the workers (proletariat) and the factory owners (bourgeoisie)."

REVOLUTION

In order to thrive, **capitalism** must create a system of **haves** and **have-nots**: the ***bourgeoisie*** (the **capitalists** who **own the factories and places of work** – the ***means of production***), and the ***proletariat*** (the **workers** who **sell their labour** and are **exploited for profit**). It is only through **changing this exploitative relationship** – through the **revolutionary overthrow of institutions** and **social relations** that **capitalist society requires** – that the **truly just communist society** can come about.

Superstructure

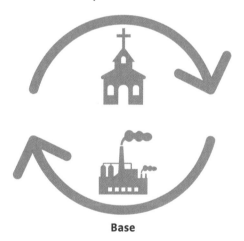

Base

OPIUM OF THE PEOPLE

The best illustration of this is Marx's famous assertion that **religion is the "opium" of the working classes**. By this, he meant that **religion reinforced the notion** that we **all have our rightful place in society**, **consoling workers** that they **must suffer in this life** so as **to enjoy an afterlife of happiness**, and **stupefying them** into **not questioning the social order**, or the **inequality** that was **built into the capitalist system**. Of course, this **reinforcing role** was also played by other things, such as the **educational system**, **newspapers**, and even **plays** and **novels**, which all **embodied values** that buttressed the **way things were**.

PRAGMATISM

C. S. Peirce argued that rather than get tied down in obscure metaphysical controversies, philosophical ideas should be weighed by their practical consequences.

 NAME CHARLES SANDERS PEIRCE

 DATES 1839–1914

 NATIONALITY AMERICAN

 SCHOOL PRAGMATISM

 MAIN WORKS "THE FIXATION OF IDEAS"; "HOW TO MAKE OUR IDEAS CLEAR"; "WHAT PRAGMATISM IS"

 KEY CONTRIBUTIONS EPISTEMOLOGY, METAPHYSICS, LOGIC

THE PRAGMATIC MAXIM

Also associated with **William James** and **John Dewey** (1859–1952), *pragmatism* is a philosophical method for gaining what **Peirce** called "**clearness of apprehension**" regarding **theoretical concepts**. What **consequences** would **believing an idea** have? If **none**, then, **regardless of whether or not your idea might be true, believing it** would seem to serve no **practical purpose**.

INTELLECTUAL TOOLS

This would seem to **reduce knowledge to practical matters**, and we can see how **such an approach may be useful in science**. But Peirce's point was that, in **evolutionary terms**, **ideas** are **tools** that we have **evolved** to **navigate** the **world**. **Francis Bacon** – who might have had sympathy for Peirce's point – put it this way: "**Knowledge is power**".

EDUCATION

A clear application of this approach can be found in **John Dewey's writings on education**, where, rather than teaching **abstract knowledge** for its own sake, or even **"employable" skills**, he advocated giving people **broader intellectual methods** of **coping with the world** that **each individual** could then **use** to **function in society**.

COHERENTISM

But what then about **truth**? Whereas **Descartes** argued that we needed a *foundation* of **absolute certainty** in order to **guarantee truth**, a **pragmatist** would consider this **unachievable**, and claim that we are better off judging beliefs according to whether they form a *coherent* whole. As such, those things that aren't "**true**" simply don't fit with the overall "**picture**". However, while this **reduces truth to what works**, this **shouldn't make us sceptical** – for what would be the use in that? Rather, it simply makes us **humble**.

FREE WILL

*Whether or not we possess free will is a question that has persisted
from the origins of philosophy down to present times.*

 NAME WILLIAM JAMES

 DATES 1842–1910

 NATIONALITY AMERICAN

 SCHOOL PRAGMATISM

 MAIN WORKS *THE WILL TO BELIEVE; THE VARIETIES OF
RELIGIOUS EXPERIENCE; PRAGMATISM; "THE DILEMMA OF
DETERMINISM"*

 KEY CONTRIBUTIONS PHILOSOPHY OF RELIGION, ETHICS,
EPISTEMOLOGY

LIBERTARIANISM

Most assume we're **free to decide how to act** (even if those actions have unpleasant **consequences**). Yet this view, known as **libertarianism (not to be confused** with the **political variety), contradicts** the **equally natural assumption** that **every event has a cause**, which, if so, means that **our actions are actually *determined*.**

DETERMINISM

There are **various forms of determinism** – social (e.g. **beliefs are formed by upbringing), biological (genes predispose obesity),** even theological (**God foreknows our future choices**). Such forms are "**hard**" or "**soft**" depending on the **degree to which we might nonetheless act differently.** I might **reject my socially inherited beliefs**, or **resist a genetic predisposition to obesity** (both arguably "soft"), but I **can't trick God** ("hard"). However, the **biggest modern challenge to libertarianism** is not **theological** but **physical**. If **every effect has a cause**, and **matter is all that exists**, then **every decision stems from** the **interaction of atoms** in the **brain, making each of my actions predetermined.** Thus ***causal determinism*** suggests that the **free will I feel is an illusion.**

COMPATIBILISM

However, some philosophers argue there's a sense in which **free will is *compatible*** with determinism. **Compatibilists** argue that I can be said to be **"free"** to do something if it is **normally within my power** and **no external force prevents me from doing so.**

PRAGMATISM

Rejecting all these approaches, pragmatist **William James** considered the question a **metaphysical** one, **beyond science's power to answer**, and therefore – like the **existence of God** or the **soul** – a matter of **personal (free?) choice**.

BELIEF

William James sought to defend religious belief against the argument that to believe without sufficient proof is to engage in irrational behaviour.

PRAGMATISM

James argued that **belief in general** is not a purely rational exercise, and that **no common beliefs** are **absolutely certain** or **supported by irrefutable fact**. Even our **confidence in our ability to complete a simple** task – such as crossing a road or hitting a ball – requires a certain amount of **"faith"**. Because such **certainty is impossible**, he argued, even **scientists** conducting **research** must adopt a ***pragmatic* attitude to belief**, exploring the **hypothesis** that, for a range of **subjective reasons**, seems to hold for them the **most promise**.

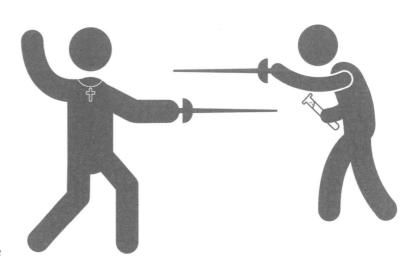

PASSIONAL NATURE

In choosing whether or not to hold a belief, James highlighted the role played by **three sets of subjective considerations**. Is the belief (1) **living** or **dead**, (2) **forced** or **avoidable**, (3) **momentous** or **trivial**? I might be **physically and mentally capable** of becoming an **astronaut**, and yet, for whatever reason – **lack of interest** in space matters, **lack of self-confidence** – it **isn't a living option for me**. Faced by a **speeding car**, the decision to move is **forced upon me**. But I can put off whether or not I choose to eat an **ice cream**, which is a **trivial concern**. What **determines these choices**? Not – or not just – our **reason**, nor any **available evidence**, but our **emotions** and **instincts**, what James calls our ***passional nature***.

THE WILL TO BELIEVE

But James is **not arguing** that **we can simply choose to believe whatever we desire to**. Like **David Hume**, he saw the **limits of reason** in **deciding our beliefs**. Nonetheless, he argued, where **evidence is insufficient to determine the answer** – as is the case with **religion** – then it is permissible that we should **follow the dictates of our emotions and instincts**.

ANARCHISM

Anarchism rejects the idea that a society requires the creation of a state to which citizens owe obedience, believing that social order is possible without traditional forms of government.

 NAME PIERRE-JOSEPH PROUDHON

 DATES 1809–56

NATIONALITY FRENCH

 SCHOOL ANARCHISM

 MAIN WORKS *WHAT IS PROPERTY?; THE PHILOSOPHY OF POVERTY*

 KEY CONTRIBUTIONS POLITICAL PHILOSOPHY

CLASSICAL ANARCHISM

Anarchism is traditionally divided into **two forms**. The **classical** or **socialist form** (we'll look at the **modern individualist form later**) originated alongside **communism** during the eighteenth century, partly as a response to the **Industrial Revolution**, but also inspired by the events of the **French Revolution**.

PROPERTY

Along with **Marx**, French philosopher **Pierre-Joseph Proudhon** rejected the notion of **private property**, arguing that such things as **land** were the **common property of society as a whole**. Marx envisaged – at least, as a temporary measure – **obedience to a centralized communist state** that **ensured equality**, and to which **everything belonged**. Instead, Proudhon argued for **personal property**, where **craftsmen** and **workers' cooperatives** should be **entitled to some degree of ownership or privileged use** of their means of production – a **carpenter** his **tools**, or **farm workers** their **fields** – as well as the **products of their own labour** – not to **sell at a profit**, but to **trade for necessary goods**. He called this economic system **Mutualism**.

MUTUAL AID

Unlike philosophers such as **Hobbes**, **Locke**, and **Rousseau**, **classical anarchists** also rejected **social contract theory**, arguing that **social order** is **possible without centralized authority**. As such, **anarchy** generally represents a more **rosy view of human nature**, stressing its **altruistic** and **communal aspects**. Accordingly, drawing on his **biological studies**, Russian anarchist philosopher **Pyotr Kropotkin** (1842–1921) argued that – from **flocks** of **birds** and **sheep**, to **beehives** and **ant colonies**, to **packs** of **wolves** – **Nature** provides numerous examples of **spontaneous cooperation**. And if humans are meant to live in **communities** (as **Aristotle** argued), then perhaps our **deepest driving instinct** is **not dominance** or **competition**, but "**mutual aid**".

NIHILISM

The German philosopher Friedrich Nietzsche famously proclaimed that "God is dead", but the true meaning of his statement is often not fully grasped.

NAME FRIEDRICH NIETZSCHE

DATES 1844–1900

NATIONALITY GERMAN

SCHOOL EXISTENTIALISM

MAIN WORKS *BEYOND GOOD AND EVIL; THUS SPAKE ZARATHUSTRA; GENEALOGY OF MORALS; THE ANTI-CHRIST*

KEY CONTRIBUTIONS ETHICS, PHILOSOPHY OF RELIGION, EPISTEMOLOGY

MEANING TO LIFE?

The word *nihilism* has various meanings, but is broadly used to denote **the belief that there is no inherent meaning to life** and that **our values have no independent foundation**. It would therefore seem that, **without God** or a **benign human nature**, there is **no basis** for the **traditional notions** of **truth**, **goodness**, or **beauty**.

GOD AND THE MADMAN

But while he is the philosopher perhaps **most often associated with nihilism**, **Nietzsche** actually spent most of his efforts **trying to provide an alternative**. He recognized that **Western culture** had begun to **move away from belief in God** – through **science** and **rationalism**, through adopting more **secular (non-religious) values** and celebrating **individualism** – but had yet to fully realize the **consequences of doing so**. And so, in *The Joyful Wisdom*, he in fact has a **madman** announce that *we have killed God* – but that we are **not yet ready for the news**, for we have **no system** or **set of values** to **put in his place**.

WHAT DOESN'T KILL ME

So **what should replace God**? Nietzsche argued that instead of bemoaning **life's meaninglessness**, we should **cultivate** and **refine** our **natural instincts**, and so **evolve our own values**. In doing this, the **highest ideal** was **not nihilistic resignation** or **Buddhist-like indifference**, but a joyful acceptance of **whatever life throws at you**.

WILL TO POWER

Nietzsche's most famous doctrine proposes that, more than an urge simply to survive, all forms of life are driven by a desire to impose their will upon the world – even philosophers.

MIGHT IS RIGHT

Will to power is often confused with the doctrine of "**might is right**", where the **strongest** and **most powerful** create a **moral code** to **justify their own dominance**. While this interpretation **isn't completely wrong**, it does suggest rather a **one-dimensional concept of "good"** – a sort of "**morality of the caveman**".

THE SLAVE REVOLT IN MORALS

But **will to power** could also operate in different ways. With the rise of **Christianity** among the **Roman poor** and **enslaved**, **pagan virtues** became **inverted**: it is not the *strong*, *wealthy*, or *powerful* that **deserve God's blessing**, but the *meek*, *poor*, and *humble*; moral justice does not consist in exacting *retribution* or *revenge*, but in *forgiveness* and *compassion*. In this way, Nietzsche argued, Christianity represents a sort of "**slave revolt**" in the **ethical world**, allowing the **inferior** to **wield** "**spiritual power**" over the **strong**. For Nietzsche, **Christian ethics** is therefore the clearest illustration that will to power can be expressed in **ingenious** and **subtle** ways – even, perhaps, **through philosophy itself**.

THE GENEALOGY OF MORALS

Nietzsche does in fact argue that **moral concepts originate in this way**. In older **pagan cultures**, such as that of **Ancient Greece** and **Rome**, "**good**" became associated with **strength**, **health**, **wealth**, and other **life-affirming qualities**, while "**bad**" was linked to **weakness**, **illness**, **poverty**, and so on. It is from these that Nietzsche traces the *genealogy* (**descent**) of our **modern ethical concepts**.

INTENTIONALITY

Intentionality is a defining feature of mental experience, and something that – arguably – only conscious beings can possess.

 NAME EDMUND HUSSERL

 DATES 1859–1938

 NATIONALITY GERMAN

SCHOOL PHENOMENOLOGY

MAIN WORKS *LOGICAL INVESTIGATIONS; CARTESIAN MEDITATIONS*

KEY CONTRIBUTIONS EPISTEMOLOGY, METAPHYSICS

CONTEMPORARY PHILOSOPHY

PHENOMENOLOGY

Intentionality is most commonly associated with *phenomenology*, a philosophical school founded by **Edmund Husserl**, drawing on the work of his teacher **Franz Brentano** (1838–1917). Instead of focusing on the **mind's relation to an independent world** (whose **true nature may be inaccessible** anyway), phenomenology concentrated on the **structure and nature of subjective experience** – mental *phenomena*. This influenced later Continental philosophers such as **Heidegger** and movements such as **existentialism** to evolve approaches that investigated **philosophical questions** in terms of **subjective human experience and being.**

ABOUTNESS

Intentionality mustn't be confused with **"intending to do"** something. **Thoughts** and **perceptions** have intentionality in terms of what they are *about*. A **mental image of my dog** isn't just a **bland, neutral snapshot** of him, but something that sees him in a **personal light** – **affectionately**, perhaps, or (if he's run off) with **consternation**. As such, mental objects are **coloured** and **shaped** by the *aboutness* of our **beliefs, desires, attitudes**, and **feelings**. We see the world in terms of our **wants** and **values**.

MINDS AND THINGS

One consequence of this is that we may consider intentionality to be an essential feature that **distinguishes minds from physical objects**. A **rock** or a **glass of water** does **not possess intentionality**. It is **only a conscious mind** that can **perceive** or **believe** or **desire** in such a way that its **mental representations possess intentionality**. But if so, then does that mean that **computers** (as physical objects) can **never possess** an **essential feature** of the **mind**? Is true **Artificial Intelligence** impossible? (We'll come back to this later.)

VITALISM

In opposition to the modern scientific conception of matter, vitalists argue that there exists a distinct force or organizing principle that distinguishes living from inanimate things.

 NAME HENRI BERGSON

 DATES 1874–1948

 NATIONALITY FRENCH

 SCHOOL CONTINENTAL PHILOSOPHY

 MAIN WORKS *CREATIVE EVOLUTION*

 KEY CONTRIBUTIONS METAPHYSICS

ANIMATING PRINCIPLES

Vitalism may be seen as an **offshoot of traditional religious, spiritual**, and **animistic conceptions** of **life**. What makes a thing "alive" is its **possession of an immaterial spirit or soul**. The **philosophical and scientific tradition** of vitalism begins with **Aristotle**, who distinguished **three types of "soul"** – **vegetable, animal**, and **rational** – that gave **each level of being** its **characteristic form** and **activity**.

MECHANISM

In more recent times, vitalism began to re-emerge in **opposition to Descartes'** *mechanistic* **view of matter**. Though Descartes too believed in **rational souls** and "**animal spirits**", he conceived of **biological matter** as *mechanistic*, requiring neither **consciousness** nor **sentience**, merely the **blind, unconscious determination of physical laws**.

ÉLAN VITAL

In contrast to **mechanism**, vitalists have argued that the **life force** has its **own inherent purpose**. For instance, the French philosopher **Henri Bergson** proposed that **Nature did not obey Darwin's mechanistic natural selection** but, imbued with *élan vital*, **spontaneously self-organized**, producing natural forms in a **creative** rather than a mechanistic way.

MODERN VITALISM

The modern vitalist tradition can be traced through **Schopenhauer's** concept of *will*, Nietzsche's *will to power*, Bergson's *élan vital*, the **postmodernism** of **Michel Foucault** and **Gilles Deleuze**, and the doctrine of *panpsychism*. It can also be found in the **psychological theories** of **Freud, Carl Jung**, and **Wilhelm Reich**. As such, vitalism often seems to represent a **fringe view**, providing **resistance to scientific** or even **political attempts** to **reduce life** – and **human beings** themselves – to a **rational principle** or **set of laws**: an **ambition** that, **vitalists argue**, can **never be achieved**.

UNDERDETERMINATION

French physicist and philosopher Pierre Duhem argued that scientific claims can't be tested singularly, but only in relation to the overall theory of which they are a part.

 NAME PIERRE DUHEM

 DATES 1861–1916

 NATIONALITY FRENCH

 SCHOOL INSTRUMENTALISM

 MAIN WORKS *THE AIM AND STRUCTURE OF PHYSICAL THEORY; TO SAVE THE PHENOMENA*

 KEY CONTRIBUTIONS PHILOSOPHY OF SCIENCE, EPISTEMOLOGY, METAPHYSICS

SAVING THE PHENOMENA

Duhem argued that, from the **Ancient Greeks** down to **Copernicus**, **science** did not concern itself so much with **describing true reality** (*realism*), but with **"preserving the phenomena"** (giving an account that **"makes sense" of events** – whatever the truth may be).

COMPETING COSMOLOGIES

According to this approach (*instrumentalism*), faced with the choice between **Ptolemy's geocentric** or **Copernicus's heliocentric views** of the universe, the **contemporary scientist** was **not concerned so much** with which is **right**, but with which presents a **more coherent story** that allows us to **predict** and **explain events** – given everything else we believe.

CONFIRMATION HOLISM

Duhem's thesis – which he had **only intended to apply to physics** – was later taken up and **extended** by **W. V. O. Quine**, who argued that **underdetermination** was a **general feature of knowledge**, and that **beliefs must be assessed not singularly but as a whole** (what he called "**confirmation holism**").

CRUCIAL EXPERIMENTS

A further consequence of this view is that **theories stand up or fall down as a whole**, and there **can be no "crucial experiments"** that can **test a single hypothesis independently of its background assumptions**. If a **sixteenth-century astronomer** made **observations** that caused **problems** for the **Ptolemaic view**, it was still possible to **patch up geocentrism** in a way that **"preserved the phenomena"** (which, for centuries, is what happened). And so, the **significance** of a **single observation** or **experiment** is **always relative** to the **bigger picture**, because the **data in themselves** *underdetermine* which theory we should adopt: we **always face a choice**.

TIME

Philosophers have long been fascinated by the nature of time, from the question of whether the future is fixed, to whether time is independent of events, or even whether time itself exists.

 NAME J. M. E. McTAGGART

 DATES 1866–1925

 NATIONALITY ENGLISH

 SCHOOL IDEALISM

 MAIN WORKS *THE UNREALITY OF TIME*

 KEY CONTRIBUTIONS METAPHYSICS

TIME AND CHANGE

Thinkers such as **Plato** and **Isaac Newton** believed that **time** was **independent of events**. So, you could have stretches of **empty time** during which **nothing happened**. If so, then (hypothetically) **aeons might pass between breathing in and out**. For such as **Aristotle** and **Leibniz**, such **"freezes"** would be **impossible**, for time was merely the **succession of events**.

TIME AND REALITY

For **John McTaggart**, time itself is **illusory**. To drastically oversimplify his argument... an event can be **past, present**, and **future**, but how can it be all **three simultaneously**? Perhaps we can say that you're **reading this *now*, will have read it** in the ***future***, and were **about to read it** in the ***past***? But this **assumes the truth of what you're trying to prove** – that past, present, and future **exist independently**. You're using the **concept of time** ... to prove the **reality of time**.

TIME AND EXISTENCE

Another **temporal puzzle** relates to the **existence of things** in the **past** or the **future**. *Presentism* assumes that **only things that are "now" exist**. But **in order to make statements about them**, doesn't there need to be a sense in which last week's storm or next week's heatwave **actually exist**? Thus, *Eternalism* argues that **past, present**, and **future continually exist**, and time is like a **spatial object** – e.g. a **road** or a **mountain** – where "past", "present" and "future" are merely **different locations** upon it. The **Growing Universe Theory** agrees, except in relation to the **future** (which **hasn't yet been created**).

MATHEMATICS

Bertrand Russell attempted to reduce mathematics to logic, but in doing so helped reveal a fundamental paradox.

 NAME BERTRAND RUSSELL

 DATES 1872–1970

 NATIONALITY BRITISH

SCHOOL ANALYTIC PHILOSOPHY

MAIN WORKS "ON DENOTING"; *PRINCIPIA MATHEMATICA; THE PROBLEMS OF PHILOSOPHY; A HISTORY OF WESTERN PHILOSOPHY*

KEY CONTRIBUTIONS LOGIC, METAPHYSICS, EPISTEMOLOGY

CLASSES

Russell's attempt was based on **set theory**. The number "1" can be thought of as the **class (set) of all single things**, the number "2" as the **class of all pairs**, and so on.

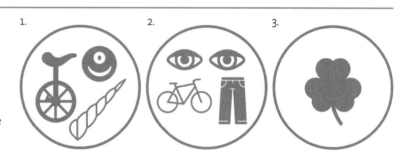

1.   2.   3.

RUSSELL'S PARADOX

But this led to **paradox**. Like **bicycle wheels** and **cyclops' eyes**, **classes are themselves things that can be classed**. We may divide **logical classes** into **two sorts**: **those that are members of themselves**, and **those that aren't**. The class of **all birds** is **not itself a bird**, but the **class of all classes is a class**. But if we create "the **class of all classes that aren't members of themselves**", then we encounter a **contradiction**. Is such a class a **member of itself** or not?

THE BARBER

To illustrate this, **Russell** proposed an **analogy**. As the **town barber**, your job is to **shave everyone who doesn't shave himself**. Do you shave **yourself**? If you don't, you should (because **it's your job to shave those who don't**); but if you do, you shouldn't (because **it's your job *only* to shave those who don't**).

INCOMPLETENESS

Russell tried to resolve the paradox by proposing that certain ***types* of class** *can't* be members of themselves. However, mathematician **Kurt Gödel** highlighted a deeper problem: a **mathematical system** will always contain **statements that cannot themselves be proven**, even though the **system relies on their truth**. Again, using a simplified popular analogy, it's **impossible to prove you aren't mad**, because **doing so requires trusting your reason**.

NON-EXISTENCE

The curious status of non-existent things had long been a puzzle to philosophers, until Russell proposed a solution.

THE PRESENT KING OF FRANCE

Russell asks us to consider the statement, "**The present King of France is bald**." Since there is no present King of France, **how do we evaluate the truth of the statement**? It seems **wrong to say it's simply false**, for in order to do so we would have to consider that there is a sense in which the present King of France exists and has no hair. But it also **doesn't appear to be meaningless**, for we can certainly **understand the statement**.

DENOTING

The problem here is that in order to be **meaningful** and to be **assessed for its truth or falsehood**, some philosophers proposed, even **fictional entities must *denote* or refer to something**. But what? The Austrian philosopher **Alexius Meinong** (1853–1920) argued that **even non-existent entities must have some form of "being"**, if not actual physical **"existence"**. But Meinong's theory would seem to commit us to a **mysterious realm of entities**, which arguably must also include **impossible yet conceivable things**.

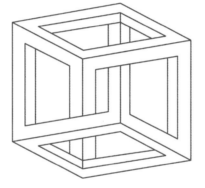

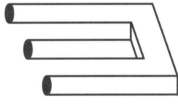

SLEIGHT OF HAND

So what's the solution? Russell argued that there is some **sleight of hand** at work here, for the **above statement is in fact not one assertion, but three**: (1) There is a person who is the present King of France, (2) who is the only present King of France, and (3) he is bald. Viewed in this way, the **statement contains an obvious falsehood**: (1) is wrong, so we don't have to worry about whether (3) is true or not. Unpacked in this way, the statement is therefore **meaningful but false**.

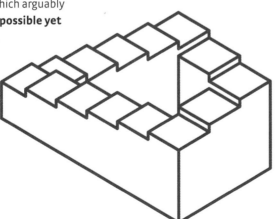

THE PROBLEM OF OTHER MINDS

Bertrand Russell argued that while we cannot be absolutely certain that other human beings have mental states in the way that we do, we may consider it highly probable.

CARTESIAN DOUBTS

The **problem of other minds** seems to stem from **Descartes**. You will recall that while he claimed he **could not doubt the existence of his own mind**, he had **no such certainty about the existence of the outside world** – or, in fact, of his **own body**. As a result, it **may be true** that **others do not possess minds like mine**, or even that **only I exist** (a view that's known as *solipsism*).

ARGUMENT FROM ANALOGY

Russell's response was to argue that my **strongest argument for assuming** that **others have mental states like my own** is from **analogy**. I can observe that **others behave in similar ways** as I do, and since my **own behaviour** is **linked to** and **caused by mental states**, then it's **reasonable to assume** that **theirs is too**. I can therefore draw an *analogy* using my **knowledge of the relationship** between my **own behaviour** and **mental states**, and **that of others**.

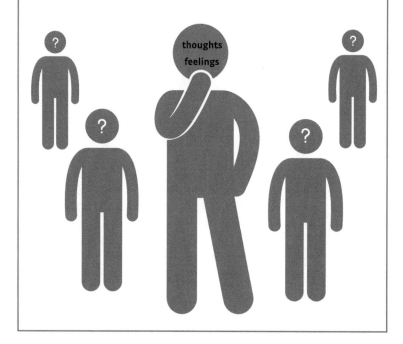

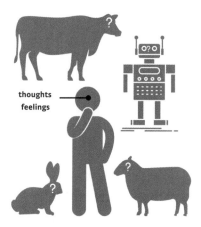

NON-HUMAN PERSONS

Perhaps the most interesting application of this problem, however, is to the **question of whether *non-humans* can possess similar mental states to our own**. Does a **dog** or an **ape** "**think**" or "**feel**" in the s**ame way a human does**? Could a **computer** or a **robot** be considered "**conscious**" or "**sentient**"? If Russell is right, then the **answer** to this question would lie in **drawing conclusions from their actions based on an understanding of our own behaviour** and its **relationship to our inner thoughts and feelings**.

STRUCTURALISM

Structuralism developed in the mid-twentieth century, drawing on the work of Swiss linguist Ferdinand de Saussure.

 NAME FERDINAND DE SAUSSURE

 DATES 1857–1913

 NATIONALITY SWISS

 SCHOOL STRUCTURALISM

 MAIN WORKS *COURSE IN GENERAL LINGUISTICS*

 KEY CONTRIBUTIONS METAPHYSICS, PHILOSOPHY OF LANGUAGE

SIGNIFIER AND SIGNIFIED

Saussure argued that **languages** were a **system of signs**. These signs were made up of the **signifier** (the **sound** or **image** that **represented something**), and the **signified** (the **idea** that the signifier pointed to).

dog
chien
cane

signifiers

signified

LANGUE AND PAROLE

Saussure explained this relationship by distinguishing between **langue** and **parole**. **Langue** refers to the **underlying rules** and **relations** that **govern a language** or **system of signs**, while **parole** denotes the **actual words** and **expressions** used **to communicate**. **Different languages and cultures** have **different parole**, but may **share the same underlying langue**. To understand a **culture**, we must therefore understand its **structure**.

INNATE LANGUAGE

Linguist **Noam Chomsky** (b.1928) would later **use structuralism** to argue that **humans possess an innate *universal grammar*** that **allows them to learn language**. For instance, we can recognize that **"Colourless green ideas sleep furiously"** (to use his famous example) is **grammatical**, even though its **content is nonsense**, because we **recognize its *structure***.

THE STRUCTURE OF STORY

Saussure's insight was taken up in **numerous fields**, and this **broad trend** became known as **structuralism**. For instance, American anthropologist **Joseph Campbell** (1904–87) employed a **structuralist approach to religion and mythology**, arguing in **The Hero with a Thousand Faces** that the **same hero figure** faced the **same tests and trials**, battling with the **same archetypes** of **gods**, **helper spirits**, and **wily antagonists** that could be **found the world over**. Famously, **George Lucas** utilised Campbell's ideas in the **Star Wars** films.

THE NATURALISTIC FALLACY

English moral philosopher G. E. Moore rejected the idea that ethical goodness should be defined as pleasure or happiness (or some other natural property).

 NAME G. E. MOORE

 DATES 1873–1958

 NATIONALITY ENGLISH

 SCHOOL ANALYTIC PHILOSOPHY

 MAIN WORKS *PRINCIPIA ETHICA*

 KEY CONTRIBUTIONS ETHICS

MOTIVATION

Moral realists consider **ethical qualities** to be in some sense **real** and **irreducible**. Moral realists are either *naturalists* or *non-naturalists*. Philosophers such as **Plato** and **Kant**, for instance, were non-naturalists: **moral qualities** are **ideas** or **principles**. By saying, "**Giving to charity is good**", I do not mean that **philanthropy gives me pleasure**, or any other natural quality (though, in addition, it might do). I mean that it's the **right thing to do**, *whatever* I feel. For **non-naturalists**, **pleasure** is therefore **incidental to moral goodness**, and to do something because it gives you a **warm feeling** inside is, strictly speaking, **not the correct motive**.

THE QUESTIONABLE GOOD

Moore's insight, however, was to see that if we **equate goodness** with some **natural quality** – pleasure, function, will to power – then we commit a **logical fallacy**. For it is always possible to say, "**Stealing** this cake will bring me **pleasure** – but is it the **right thing to do**?" But **if goodness *is* simply pleasure** (or whatever), then this question is an **empty one**.

MORAL NATURALISM

In **opposition to moral non-naturalism**, **moral naturalism** proposes that "**goodness**" can in fact be translated into some **natural quality**. For instance, **Jeremy Bentham** argued that "**good**" was in fact **pleasure**, and being **happy** therefore involved **maximizing** that. In contrast, **Thomas Aquinas's** doctrine of *natural law* proposed that **human happiness** depended on **fulfilling our proper natural "function"**, which in turn depended on **God's purpose in creating our natures**. But both approaches, in their different ways, are **naturalistic**, for they relate **moral goodness** to a **natural property**.

FORMALISM

Formalism views art purely in terms of form and structure, in relation to which other elements are less important or even irrelevant.

 NAME CLIVE BELL

 DATES 1881–1964

 NATIONALITY ENGLISH

 SCHOOL FORMALISM

 MAIN WORKS *ART*

 KEY CONTRIBUTIONS AESTHETICS

KANT

Perhaps the first to propose a **formalist theory of art** was **Kant** in his ***Critique of Judgment***, who argued that the **key elements** of a **work of art** are such things as **shape** and **line** (in **visual art**), and **structure** (in **literature** or **music**). Other **non-formal elements**, such as a painting's **colour**, merely add "**charm**" to a piece.

SIGNIFICANT FORM

In the **visual arts**, especially **painting**, this view was developed by **Clive Bell**, whose notion of ***significant form*** saw art as conveying an ***aesthetic emotion*** through its use of **line**, **form**, **colour**, and **composition**. Such emotion was **distinct from any reactions arising to the subject depicted** (assuming it to be **representational art**), and the emotions raised **need not be beautiful** or **noble**.

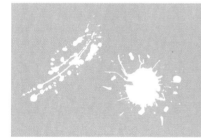

ABSTRACT EXPRESSIONISM

This formalist approach can also be found in the writings of art critic **Clement Greenberg**, who championed the ***action painting*** of **Jackson Pollock**. Here, painting is **reduced** to formal, ***abstract elements*** (which often **do not "represent" anything**) in order to **express emotion**.

CONTEXT

Controversially, formalism argues that **we don't need to venture outside an artwork to understand it**. As a consequence, any **external associations** or **references** related to the artwork can be **ignored**. But while this may work with **painting** or **music**, it seems to present **a special challenge** for works of **literature**, which often contain **historical** and **cultural references**. Can we fully appreciate **James Joyce's** *Ulysses* via its use of **metaphor** or **verbal style** alone, without reference to the **history of Ireland**?

BEING

The philosophy of Martin Heidegger is fundamentally concerned with ontology – the nature of Being – the essential puzzle of which he claimed philosophers to date had largely ignored.

 NAME MARTIN HEIDEGGER

 DATES 1889–1976

 NATIONALITY GERMAN

 SCHOOL EXISTENTIAL PHENOMENOLOGY

 MAIN WORKS *BEING AND TIME*

 KEY CONTRIBUTIONS METAPHYSICS

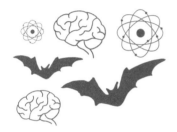

ONTOLOGY

Ontology is a branch of **metaphysics**, and as such concerns the **fundamental nature of what exists.** When we imagine **what it's like to be a bat, whether the universe ultimately consists of one thing or many, or if mind is separate from body,** then we are **seeking answers to ontological questions.**

DASEIN

While philosophers had always been concerned with **certain types of ontological question**, **Heidegger** thought the **deeper problem** – the **nature of Being itself** – remained **unsolved.** Drawing on the ideas of his teacher **Edmund Husserl** (discussed earlier), he took a *phenomenological* approach, considering subjectively *what it's like* for beings such as we are to exist. Unlike animals, **humans possess unique awareness of their own existence, mortality,** and **need for meaning** – a perspective he terms *Dasein* ("being-there").

"BEING-IN-THE-WORLD"

In this, Heidegger pioneered an approach that was **later to influence existentialist philosophy.** *Dasein* finds itself **not as a spectator at a play,** but born already onstage, expected to fulfil a role. But for Heidegger, there is **no such division** – no "**subject**" and "**object**" – for our experience of existence is of *being-in-the-world*, a state that already **presupposes** **our part in things**, and that **shapes** and **colours** the **nature of our consciousness**.

"BEING-TOWARDS-DEATH"

But **what, then, is the meaning of the play, or our role in it?** Heidegger **doesn't supply any easy answers**, but **does suggest how we might find our own:** by **adopting an attitude** – a *being-towards-death* – we may **remember that we are finite, mortal creatures**, whose **being is shaped by time**, and thus live an *authentic*, meaningful life.

EXPRESSIONISM

The expressionism of R. G. Collingwood proposes that, unlike craft, true art is not the means to some preconceived ends, but a spontaneous form of imaginative expression.

 NAME R. G. COLLINGWOOD

 DATES 1889–1943

 NATIONALITY ENGLISH

 SCHOOL IDEALISM

 MAIN WORKS *THE PRINCIPLES OF ART*

 KEY CONTRIBUTIONS AESTHETICS

EMOTION

Different varieties of this view have been advanced by Italian philosopher **Benedetto Croce** (1866–1952) and Russian novelist **Leo Tolstoy**, but it was **most fully developed** by English philosopher **R. G. Collingwood**. Like **formalism**, **expressionism** (or **expressivism**) argues that the **value of art** lies in expression of **emotion**, **not in any ideas it conveys**. However, unlike formalism, expressionism **does not restrict itself** to the **formal aspects** of an artwork.

TRUE ART

Collingwood argues that art is **often confused with other things**. There may be **artistry** in a **watchmaker's skill**, or in a talented **painter's ability** to **photorealistically depict a scene**. There may be art in the promotion of **political**, **social**, or **religious purposes**, or even where something is created primarily for **entertainment**. But **true art does not aim at any of these things**, which Collingwood merely considers to be "**craft**", and which **express emotion for a pre-existing purpose** (whatever that is).

IMAGINATIVE EXPRESSION

In contrast to craft, **true art** happens when ***imaginative expression*** gives **embodiment** to **previously unconscious feelings**. In this, Collingwood comes close to the traditional notion of "**inspiration**", though he **rejects the idea** of the **sole artistic genius**: artistic **creation** is a **collaboration**, **channelling** and **combining influences** from across the **artist's life** and **social relationships**. The **audience** plays **as much of a role** in the **creation of the play** as the **actors** and **playwright** do.

SAYING AND SHOWING

Wittgenstein attempted to reveal the relationship of language to the world, and in so doing argued that there are limits to what philosophers can say before descending into nonsense.

 NAME LUDWIG WITTGENSTEIN

 DATES 1889–1951

 NATIONALITY AUSTRIAN

 SCHOOL ANALYTIC PHILOSOPHY

 MAIN WORKS *TRACTATUS LOGICO-PHILOSOPHICUS; PHILOSOPHICAL INVESTIGATIONS*

 KEY CONTRIBUTIONS PHILOSOPHY OF LANGUAGE, LOGIC, EPISTEMOLOGY, METAPHYSICS

PICTURE THEORY

Wittgenstein's philosophical career is often divided into **two periods**. He developed his **early philosophical ideas** under the **mentorship** of **Bertrand Russell**, working in the so-called **analytic tradition** that had seen philosophy focus on **language** (sometimes called *the linguistic turn*), while his **later work** marks a **fundamental shift in direction**. The **early Wittgenstein** attempted to show that there was a **logical structure to the world** that was **revealed in language**. By making **statements**, we make **"pictures"** consisting of **various combinations** of "logical atoms" that **either do or do not correspond to reality**.

THE FLY IN THE BOTTLE

While he **later abandoned aspects of this theory**, one theme seems to remain **constant**. There are **truths about the nature of the world** that **cannot be meaningfully spoken about**; they can only be "**shown**". For instance, I can show you the **rules of a game**, or give examples of **how grammar works**. But in any explanation, there comes a point where we simply say, "Well, that's **just the way things are**", where to go **beyond that point** risks talking **nonsense**. The **philosopher's job**, as Wittgenstein saw it, was therefore **to help us avoid such nonsense**. His **later work** would put this more **forcefully**, seeing **philosophy** merely as a **set of puzzles and confusions**, released from which – rather **like a fly that has been trapped in a bottle** – we are **free to concentrate on the "real" problem of how to live**.

PRIVATE LANGUAGE

Wittgenstein's later philosophy concentrates on the public nature of language, arguing that how we understand the world – even our private selves – is dependent on being part of a community.

AYER'S CRUSOE

Imagine that, **instead of being stranded** on a desert island **as an adult**, Robinson Crusoe had **grown up there alone**. Would he have **evolved his own language**? When "Friday" showed up, would Crusoe have been able to **name him**? In a discussion with English philosopher **A. J. Ayer**, **Wittgenstein** argued that he **could not have done** that. Ayer saw no obstacle to Crusoe simply choosing his own "**labels**" for things – evolving his own **private language** – but Wittgenstein pointed out that even the notion of "**labelling**" was something we learn as part of a **language community**, and that **language learning itself** is something that **requires others**. Without such a community, Crusoe would not only have been **inarticulate**, but would have lacked any sort of **sophisticated thought**. He would have been **close to an animal**.

THE BEETLE IN THE BOX

We may further understand Wittgenstein's point if we consider the curious analogy of the **beetle in the box**. Imagine, Wittgenstein says, that each of us has a box with a beetle in it, but that **no one is allowed to look in anyone else's box. How do I know that my beetle resembles yours**? Since each person's beetle in this scenario can **only be viewed by its owner**, the word "beetle" as it's used **publicly** simply comes to mean "**whatever's in my box**". This strange analogy is meant to illustrate that **even our "private" thoughts depend on a publicly shared language** (beetle = private self). What I think of as **myself** is really something that I've **learned to describe** through terms I've acquired as a member of a **language community**. If I had no **public words** to describe my **innermost self**, **would I even have one**? Wittgenstein isn't saying we'd have no *perceptions*, of course; merely that we **wouldn't be able to describe or possibly even think about them**.

THE PARADOX OF CONFIRMATION

Modern scientists accept that their theories cannot be proven conclusively. However, C. G. Hempel argued that there is even a problem regarding the evidence that supports a hypothesis.

 NAME CARL GUSTAV HEMPEL

 DATES 1905–97

 NATIONALITY GERMAN

 SCHOOL ANALYTIC PHILOSOPHY

 MAIN WORKS *STUDIES IN THE LOGIC OF CONFIRMATION*

 KEY CONTRIBUTIONS EPISTEMOLOGY, LOGIC

SCIENTIFIC UNCERTAINTY

As the **problem of induction** makes clear, because scientific theories rely on **observation** and **amassing of evidence**, they **cannot be absolutely certain**. Hypothesis X may be **true today**, but **tomorrow** we may **discover a fact** that **contradicts it**, or **another hypothesis** that **better accounts for the evidence**. All scientific theories are therefore merely **provisional**. However, the **more evidence** we have **in support of a theory**, the *higher the degree of confirmation* it has, and the **more likely it is to be true**.

BLACK RAVENS

Let us suppose that I believe that "All ravens are black." Every black raven I see will add to the **evidence** I have in **support of this statement**, making it **stronger** and **less likely to be wrong**.

 = all ravens are black

INDOOR ORNITHOLOGY

However, it's **not just positive confirmation** that makes a **hypothesis stronger**. If it's true that "All ravens are black", then the **opposite is also true**: "All non-black things are not ravens." Hempel therefore reasoned that every time we see something that is not a black raven, our belief that all ravens are black is strengthened. But this is **absurd**, for it means that (for instance) seeing a yellow car, or a blue shirt, or a green ball also counts as evidence in support of "all ravens are black". In fact, I could practise "indoor ornithology" by just staying at home and merely noting all the non-black non-ravens I see around me. Couldn't I?

THE NEW RIDDLE OF INDUCTION

A further problem for scientific knowledge was proposed by Nelson Goodman, who argued that it was not sufficient that an inductive argument be valid.

 NAME NELSON GOODMAN

 DATES 1906–98

 NATIONALITY AMERICAN

 SCHOOL ANALYTIC PHILOSOPHY

 MAIN WORKS *FACT, FICTION AND FORECAST*

 KEY CONTRIBUTIONS EPISTEMOLOGY, LOGIC

WELL-FORMED INDUCTION

Despite discovering the **Raven Paradox**, **Hempel**, and philosophers such as **Rudolf Carnap** (1891–1970), hoped to bring **induction** in line with **deduction**. You may recall that **deductive arguments** are *sound* if their **premises are true**, and the **form** of the argument is *valid* (**obeys the rules of logic**). While **inductive arguments can never be certain**, couldn't we at least establish **what form they should take** in order to give them the **highest degree of probability**?

"**Premise**: All emeralds ever seen have been green; **Conclusion**: all as yet unobserved emeralds will be green."

GRUE

This hope was torpedoed by **Nelson Goodman**, who pointed out that you could have two **equally well-formed inductive arguments**, where one of which is **highly unlikely**. Imagine, Goodman said, that we **create a new colour**, "Grue", which can be defined as "everything that has ever been observed that's green, or everything yet to be observed that's blue". This may seem an odd concept, but Goodman is using it to make a particular point.

green things observed in past   blue things not yet observed

BLUE EMERALDS

Now, previously observed green things – all emeralds, leaves, etc., ever seen – will also be "grue". But it seems **hugely unlikely** that the next emerald I see will be blue. The **argument would therefore seem weak** – and yet it takes the *identical form* as the **much more likely argument** that "All emeralds ever seen are green; therefore all future emeralds will be green." In other words, **likely and unlikely inductive arguments cannot be distinguished merely in terms of how well they are formed**.

CONSUMERISM

Herbert Marcuse argued that, rather than reflecting a new world of free choice and wealth, the consumerism of modern democratic societies embodied a form of totalitarian control.

 NAME HERBERT MARCUSE

 DATES 1898–1979

 NATIONALITY GERMAN-AMERICAN

 SCHOOL CONTINENTAL PHILOSOPHY (MARXISM/FRANKFURT SCHOOL)

 MAIN WORKS *EROS AND CIVILISATION; ONE-DIMENSIONAL MAN*

 KEY CONTRIBUTIONS POLITICAL PHILOSOPHY, SOCIAL THEORY

THE END OF CLASS STRUGGLE

Marcuse's philosophy is essentially an **update of Marxism**. He recognized that the **affluence** allowed by **consumerist society** had undermined the **traditional class struggle of haves** and **have-nots**, allowing energies that would otherwise fuel **political discontent** to be **channelled** into **pleasures** and **possessions**.

PURCHASING HAPPINESS

Through this process, **consumers** came to **identify** with the **material objects** that they were **trained to desire**, considering the **cars** and **cookers** and **TVs** almost as **extensions of themselves**, and as **indications of their personal worth**.

TOTALITARIANISM WITHOUT TEARS

By **distracting** its members with **pleasures** and **possessions**, **democracies** could achieve a subtle form of **social control**. You **work constantly** to meet the "**false desires**" that **consumerist society implants** in you. These "**needs**" are **constantly replenished** by the **built-in obsolescence** of the **products you consume**, as you **throw away** each **TV** or **car** or **cooker** to **buy better ones**. But this **masks the fact** that such societies are **no less oppressive** than **communist** or **fascist dictatorships**, merely practising a form of *repressive tolerance*, apparently allowing you to **believe** and **behave as you want** – as long as you **don't rock the consumer system** itself.

THE GREAT REFUSAL

What, then, is the **answer**? Marcuse argued that we needed a *great refusal*, whereby people begin to **turn their back** on the **false happiness of consumerism**, and to **critically engage** with the **lifestyle** that it promotes.

SPONTANEOUS ORDER

Friedrich Hayek believed that just as natural selection explained natural order, true social and economic order required no central planner or designer, but spontaneously emerged.

 NAME FRIEDRICH HAYEK

 DATES 1899–1992

 NATIONALITY AUSTRIAN

 SCHOOL ANALYTIC PHILOSOPHY

 MAIN WORKS *THE ROAD TO SERFDOM; INDIVIDUALISM AND ECONOMIC ORDER*

 KEY CONTRIBUTIONS POLITICAL PHILOSOPHY, EPISTEMOLOGY

PRICE SIGNALS

Like **Adam Smith**, **Hayek** believed that **free markets** were **key to economic prosperity**: without **central planning**, markets **self-regulate**, and much **more efficiently** and **quickly** than any **controlling body** could effect. For example, a **global shortage of steel** will be **reflected in the price**, informing canny buyers to look for **substitutes** or **produce their own**. So, as long as no **centralized power** keeps the cost **artificially high** (or **low**), then the various **buyers**, **sellers**, **manufacturers**, etc., can act accordingly, using the ***price signals*** as **real-time information**.

SCEPTICAL FREEDOM

But **spontaneous order** was not just a feature of **markets**, but also of **social and political order**. In this regard, Hayek identified **two general traditions**. The ***sceptical tradition*** emphasized the **limitations of human knowledge**, and thus allowed room for **innovation**, and **trial and error**, where order was **not the result of deliberate human design**, but evolved and **self-adjusted spontaneously**. A **modern decentralized Western democracy** such as the USA would be an example, here, where there is (mostly) **minimal governmental interference**.

RATIONAL TYRANNY

In contrast, the ***rationalist tradition*** emphasized the human capacity to **acquire knowledge** and use it to **plan** and **control**. Historically, the **Soviet Union** would be a prime example of this approach, where **almost every aspect of social and economic life** was **determined centrally by state policy**. So, whereas, for Hayek, the **sceptical approach** fostered **true individuality** and **freedom**, the **rationalist approach** created a **false individuality**, as **totalitarian authority** forced people into **collective roles** that **imposed uniform equality**.

BEHAVIOURISM

Although B. F. Skinner was a psychologist, his concept of the human being as a biological machine whose behaviour could be programmed influenced theories in both philosophy of mind and education.

 NAME B. F. SKINNER

 DATES 1904–90

 NATIONALITY AMERICAN

 SCHOOL BEHAVIOURISM

 MAIN WORKS *THE BEHAVIOUR OF ORGANISMS; WALDEN TWO; VERBAL BEHAVIOUR*

 KEY CONTRIBUTIONS PHILOSOPHY OF MIND

PSYCHODYNAMISM

Building on the work of Russian physiologist **Ivan Pavlov**, behaviourism developed largely as a **reaction against** the **psychodynamic psychology** of **Sigmund Freud** and his followers. For such as Freud, the **mind** was to be **understood** in terms of the **interaction** of **conscious** and **unconscious forces**. As such, it contained **private, subjective events** that could only be **accessed** through a person's **own introspection** (**looking within**), that person then **reporting** those **thoughts** and **feelings** to a **psychologist** to be **interpreted** and **analysed**.

Psychodynamic psychology

OPERANT CONDITIONING

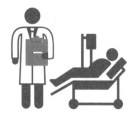

The **scientific method** of **Skinner** and other psychologists (*methodological behaviourism*) also influenced a **philosophical theory of mind** (*logical* or *analytical behaviourism*), which we look at later. But, by attempting to show **how easily** our **behaviour** can be **influenced by positive or negative reinforcement** (*operant conditioning*), Skinner also **undermined** the **philosophical concept** of **free will**. Our **beliefs** and **actions** are **not rational free choices**, but simply the result of **conditioning**. We are merely **biological machines** programmed by **genes**, **experience**, and **environment**.

OBSERVABLE BEHAVIOUR

In contrast, behaviourism – as the name implies – **reduced mental events** to **physically observable behaviour**. A **depressed person** displays certain **physical symptoms: decreased heart rate, slumped posture, lowered gaze**, etc. Similarly, to **think** or **believe** something is merely to be **liable to behave in a certain way** should the **occasion arise**: to believe that a **certain author is good** would mean that I will **likely buy their new book** if I see it in a bookshop. In this focus on **objective** and **measurable events**, behaviourism attempted to **transform psychology** into a **science**.

VERIFICATIONISM

A. J. Ayer argued that only statements justified by logic or backed up by experience could be considered meaningful.

 NAME ALFRED JULES AYER

 DATES 1910–89

 NATIONALITY ENGLISH

 SCHOOL LOGICAL POSITIVISM, ANALYTIC PHILOSOPHY

 MAIN WORKS *LANGUAGE, TRUTH, AND KNOWLEDGE; THE PROBLEM OF KNOWLEDGE*

 KEY CONTRIBUTIONS EPISTEMOLOGY, METAPHYSICS

THE VERIFICATION PRINCIPLE

Drawing on **Hume** and the early **Wittgenstein**, **Ayer** was for a time a key figure in *logical positivism*, a **controversial** and **short-lived movement** that wished to **set philosophy on a new footing**, **freeing** it from **unprovable assertions** and **metaphysical claptrap**. Many statements, Ayer argued, were neither **logically justified** nor **empirically verifiable**. This he called the ***verification principle***.

TAUTOLOGIES

A **logical truth** is a ***tautology*** – i.e. **saying the same thing twice**. "**All circles are round**" doesn't say anything **new**, because circles are, **by definition**, round things. It's the same as saying, "**All round things are round things**", which is equivalent to "**A = A**". The **same goes for maths**: "12 = 4 + 8" is really telling us about the meaning of "12" (that it is the same as "4 + 8").

PROBLEMS OF PROOF

If not **tautologies**, then **meaningful statements** must be **verifiable by experience**. This sounds very scientific, but it **quickly runs into difficulties**. **Modern physics** hypothesizes about the **existence of particles** it can only **infer indirectly** from **experiments**. Are such particles "**verified**" by such "**observations**"? And when does *enough* observation count as **proof**? Think of the **problem of induction**. And what of the **verification principle** itself, which seems **neither tautologous nor verifiable**?

THE OPEN SOCIETY

In defending the notion of a liberal and democratic society, Karl Popper highlighted the dangerous totalitarianism hidden in the ideas of some of the great philosophers.

LIBERAL DEMOCRACY

First introduced by French philosopher **Henri Bergson**, the ideal of the **open society** may be opposed to that of a **"closed" society** ruled by **unquestioned tradition** and **authoritarian dogma**. In *The Open Society and Its Enemies*, **Popper** developed this idea, arguing that the philosophies of **Plato**, **Hegel**, and **Marx** were actually the **inspiration for totalitarianism repression**.

PHILOSOPHER KINGS

Popper sees **Plato's ideal republic** as fundamentally **undemocratic**, **elitist**, and **repressive**, where its members are **coerced** and **manipulated** into **rigid roles** on the basis of what is essentially a **lie** (that we are **all born to fulfil different social functions**). Rather than bowing to the **"wisdom"** of Plato's **philosopher kings**, he argued, a **truly just society should allow critical debate** and **respect individual freedom**.

HISTORICAL DESTINY

Popper's next target is **Hegel**, whose *teleological* **view of history** he critiques. There is, he argues, **no destined end goal** that historical events follow, and the belief in some sort of **historical destiny** leads us to place our trust in some **dubious metaphysical notion** of **how things "must" play out**.

MARX

While **Popper** recognizes **Marx's great sympathy** for the plight of the **oppressed**, he sees him as possessed by the same spirit as **Hegel**. In fact, one of the key insights of Popper's book is the way in which it reveals how both **fascists** and **communists** have been driven by the **same Hegelian belief in historical destiny**, which they have seized upon in seeking to **justify oppression** and **persecution**.

CATEGORY MISTAKES

Taking issue with Cartesian dualism, Gilbert Ryle argued that the idea that we possess a mind or self distinct from our physical capacities and behaviour is a form of logical error.

 NAME GILBERT RYLE

 DATES 1900–76

 NATIONALITY ENGLISH

 SCHOOL ANALYTICAL BEHAVIOURISM

 MAIN WORKS *THE CONCEPT OF MIND*

 KEY CONTRIBUTIONS PHILOSOPHY OF MIND

THE GHOST IN THE MACHINE

One **solution** to the **problem of interaction** created by **Descartes' dualism** is simply to **do away with the non-physical part**. This, largely, is what **modern philosophers have done**, in different ways. **Gilbert Ryle** argued that **dualism created a false picture** of **what it is to be a person**, treating the **mind** as a sort of **"ghost in the machine"** (to use his famous phrase).

OXFORD UNIVERSITY

Ryle pointed out that looking for a thing called **"mind" separate from the physical manifestations** of my ability to **speak**, **think**, **create**, **act**, etc., was rather like being shown all the **buildings that make up Oxford University**, and then **asking to see the University itself**. This, Ryle argued, is a *category mistake*, assuming that "**university**" is an additional thing, existing in the **same category** of **physical things** as the **buildings** that **make it up**.

PROBLEMS OF PROOF

Instead, Ryle argued that **mental concepts** can be **understood** or **analysed** in terms of our actual or **potential behaviour**, a position which has therefore become known as ***analytical behaviourism***. To say someone is **angry** is not to say that they have an **internal state**, but that they may **punch you if provoked**. To say that I believe it will rain may mean that I'm carrying an umbrella. In this way, what is "**internal**" becomes "**external**", thus **doing away with** the need for **spiritual essences**.

AUTHENTICITY

Faced with absolute freedom regarding how we should live our lives, Jean-Paul Sartre nonetheless argued that some choices are authentic, while others are acts of bad faith.

 NAME JEAN-PAUL SARTRE

 DATES 1905–80

 NATIONALITY FRENCH

 SCHOOL EXISTENTIALISM

 MAIN WORKS *EXISTENTIALISM AND HUMANISM; BEING AND NOTHINGNESS; NAUSEA*

 KEY CONTRIBUTIONS ETHICS, POLITICAL PHILOSOPHY

CONTEMPORARY PHILOSOPHY

EXISTENCE AND ESSENCE

As an **atheist**, Sartre thought that there was **no God** to whom we **owed allegiance**, or who **created us with a purpose**. But nor, he believed, were we defined by **human nature**. In **Sartre**'s terms, our **existence** precedes our **essence**. Unlike a watch or a car, or any other **manmade device**, we have **no creator** to define our *essence*, and we are therefore, in **existential terms**, *condemned to be free*; free to **choose not only how to live**, but **what our life means for us**.

BAD FAITH

Nonetheless, while we are **free to choose**, it is **still possible to make choices that** in some way *deny* **that freedom**, what Sartre terms an act of *bad faith*. If I blame my **violent temper** on my **natural disposition** (such as **medieval astrologers** did), I am in effect making an **excuse**, giving up **responsibility for my actions** in return for a **meaning imposed by an outside force or system of thought**. In contrast, **existentialism argues** that while **not everything that happens** to you will be **under your control, you always have the freedom on how you choose to react to circumstances**.

THE EXISTENTIALIST TRADITION

While the term is often associated with him, **Sartre did not originate many of the ideas and concepts** that **we now associate with existentialism**, but he and others developed them from earlier thinkers with **"existentialist" traits**.

EXISTENTIALIST THINKERS

Arthur Schopenhauer (1788–1860)
Friedrich Nietzsche (1844–1900)
Søren Kierkegaard (1813–55)
Martin Heidegger (1889–1976)
Jean-Paul Sartre (1905–80)
Albert Camus (1913–60)
Simone de Beauvoir (1908–86)

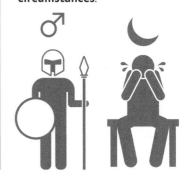

TOTALITARIANISM

As a German Jew, Hannah Arendt witnessed first-hand the rise of Nazism, and her philosophy is dedicated to understanding the nature of totalitarianism and the true meaning of political freedom.

 NAME HANNAH ARENDT

 DATES 1906–75

 NATIONALITY GERMAN

 SCHOOL EXISTENTIALISM; PHENOMENOLOGY

 MAIN WORKS *THE ORIGINS OF TOTALITARIANISM; THE HUMAN CONDITION; EICHMANN IN JERUSALEM*

 KEY CONTRIBUTIONS POLITICAL PHILOSOPHY

POLITICAL ENGAGEMENT

For **Arendt**, the **cornerstone of political freedom** was **not a community based on shared values or traditions**, but **one that encouraged engagement**. Like **Aristotle**, she thought that a society was **best protected from corruption** and **oppression** when **citizens played their full part** in its **political life**.

VITA ACTIVA

In their **practical activities** – what Arendt termed the ***vita activa*** (**active life**) – human beings **engage with the world in three ways**: through **labour**, **work**, and **action**. As with **animals**, the "labour" of **acquiring food** and **shelter** ensures our **basic biological survival**. A **step above this**, "work" involves the **productive activity** required to **create** and **maintain material conditions suitable for human beings**. But it is **only through their powers of agency** – "action" – that **humans express themselves** to their **fullest potential** as beings with **rationality**, **identity**, and **moral integrity**.

UNIFORMITY AND SUBMISSION

In contrast to this, Arendt saw **Hitler's Nazi Germany** and **Stalin's Communist Russia** as moving in the **opposite direction** to this ideal. Instead of helping to **realize distinct individual identity** and **rationality**, such **totalitarian regimes** sought to **reduce individuals** to a **uniform mass** adhering to a **single tradition** or **set of beliefs**. In doing so, Hitler and Stalin attempted to **terrorize into submission** not just **political enemies**, but the **population as a whole**, and therefore **quash** any "**dissent**" – something that Arendt saw as a sign of a **healthy** and **free society** – thus **reducing** the **active life** to one of **unthinking labour**.

THE OTHER

The concept of alterity – "otherness" – appears in various philosophical contexts, from the development of self-consciousness, cultural and sexual identity, to ethical obligation.

 NAME EMMANUEL LEVINAS

 DATES 1906–95

 NATIONALITY LITHUANIAN

 SCHOOL EXISTENTIAL PHENOMENOLOGY

 MAIN WORKS *TOTALITY AND INFINITY; ALTERITY AND TRANSCENDENCE*

 KEY CONTRIBUTIONS ETHICS, METAPHYSICS

LORD AND BONDSMAN

In his myth of "**Lord and Bondsman**" (sometimes translated **"master and slave"**), **Hegel** saw **recognition of the Other** as a **vital stage** in the **growth of self-consciousness** – whether the **psychological development** of an **individual**, of **one race** or **nation** in **relation to another**, or some other context. Initially, the Other represents a **challenge** or **limit** to a **subject's freedom**, resulting in a **struggle for dominance**, but the **tensions** within this **relationship** force it to **evolve**, ultimately facilitating **mutual recognition** and **self-consciousness**.

FACE TO FACE

Lithuanian-born philosopher **Emmanuel Levinas** applied **alterity** to ethics. **The Other** forces us to **question who we think we are** – the **Self** or "**I**" – and sets **ethical boundaries**. In this, Levinas argues, it is the **face itself** – the **outward expression** of **thought** and **feeling** in **another person** – that **obliges us to admit** that **the Other** is **not a mere object for exploitation** but **a being to which we are accountable**. It is therefore this *face-to-face* encounter that is the **foundation of morality**, and **reveals ethics itself** – not metaphysics or epistemology – to be the **true foundation of philosophy**.

THE GAZE

Jean-Paul Sartre used **alterity** as a **solution** to the **problem of other minds** (discussed previously): spying through a keyhole, we hear a noise behind us, and are suddenly **ashamed**, experiencing ourselves as the *object* of another's gaze. The notion of **objectification** also forms part of the concept of the "**male gaze**" identified by feminist film theorist **Laura Mulvey**, where **women on screen** are **sexualized** and **stereotyped** by **male directors** and **filmmakers**.

NATURALISM

Naturalism in philosophy is the general belief that the physical world is all that exists, and that we should therefore only seek explanations in natural terms.

 NAME WILLARD VAN ORMAN QUINE

 DATES 1908–2000

 NATIONALITY AMERICAN

 SCHOOL ANALYTIC

 MAIN WORKS "TWO DOGMAS OF EMPIRICISM"; *WORD AND OBJECT*

 KEY CONTRIBUTIONS EPISTEMOLOGY, METAPHYSICS, LOGIC

EMPIRICISM

Naturalism may apply to **any topic** – **ethics**, **religion**, **psychology** – and in seeking **natural explanations** for phenomena, **science itself** is **broadly naturalist**. Thus, naturalism has **strong ties** to the *empiricist* belief that **all knowledge is ultimately based on sensory evidence**.

NATURALIZED EPISTEMOLOGY

A pioneer of this view was **W. V. O. Quine**, who **applied naturalism to *epistemology* (theory of knowledge)** and **philosophy of science**, arguing that **empiricism** (as philosophers had **so far employed it**) had **not yet gone far enough** and still contained **unjustified beliefs** (*dogmas*).

WEB OF BELIEF

But how do we define "**analytic**"? If we say "bachelor" and "unmarried man" are *synonymous* (**mean the same thing**), then **how should we define "synonymy"?** If we say synonymous terms can **always be substituted for one another**, then this **simply isn't true** – in the phrase, "*bachelor* is an eight-letter word", we can't **substitute** "unmarried man" without **changing the meaning**. Through these and other examples, Quine argues that even such **basic ideas** are **not simple** and **independent**, but **rely on each other** for their **meaning** and **truth** – they exist in a *web of belief*, where even **fundamental concepts** may be **subject to change**.

ANALYTIC–SYNTHETIC DISTINCTION

One such dogma is **Kant's distinction between** *analytic* statements, which are **true by virtue of their meaning**, and *synthetic* statements, which **depend on** the **way the world is**. "All bachelors are unmarried" is true merely by *analysing* the **statement itself** ("bachelor" means "unmarried man"), but "Jim is a bachelor" is something I **need to check** (Jim may have recently married).

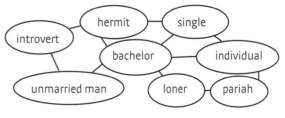

CONCEPTUAL SCHEMES

Quine's naturalism also led him to sceptical and relativist views about language: that it is impossible to know not only what others mean, but even – in a sense – what we ourselves do.

INDETERMINACY OF TRANSLATION

While studying a **remote**, **non-English-speaking tribe**, an **anthropologist** sees one of the natives point to a **rabbit** and say, "**gavagai**". "Ah," he thinks, "he **means 'rabbit'**." But **does he?** Perhaps he means "**there's a rabbit**", or the abstract noun "**rabbitness**", or a verb ("**it's rabbiting**"), or even (more strangely) "**undetatched rabbit parts**" (that is, all the limbs and ears, etc., **assembled together in one place**).

gavagai

rabbit

SAPIR–WHORF HYPOTHESIS

These possibilities may sound **peculiar**, but Quine's point is that in **trying to understand him**, the **anthropologist makes certain background assumptions** about the **native's language** and his **view of the world** – e.g. **"gavagai" is the name of a thing** – thereby **imposing his own *conceptual scheme***. A **related hypothesis** was put forward by anthropologist **Edward Sapir** (1884–1939) and linguist **Benjamin Lee Whorf** (1897–1941), who argued that people **don't simply speak different languages**, but may have evolved **different fundamental ideas about reality**. Thus, Whorf alleged that the **Hopi Indians** possess a **concept of time radically different** to the **Western linear notion** of **past**, **present**, and **future**.

INSCRUTABILITY OF REFERENCE

Quine's point, though, is **deeper** and **more sceptical** than this, for such **difficulties in translation** do not simply occur between **different languages**, but between **speakers** of the **same language**, and even in relation to what a **single individual thinks he means**. The problem isn't that such meanings are **hidden** or "**inscrutable**", but that there simply *isn't* **one essential underlying truth** that **determines what "gavagai"** (or "*lapin*", or "rabbit") ***actually* refers to**. Rather, **language is simply a net of interrelated concepts**, and it is this **overall scheme of similarities and differences that produces meaning**.

FEMINISM

While first-wave feminism sought to give women equal legal and political rights, second-wave feminism sought broader social goals.

 NAME SIMONE DE BEAUVOIR

 DATES 1908–86

 NATIONALITY FRENCH

 SCHOOL EXISTENTIALISM/FEMINISM

 MAIN WORKS *THE SECOND SEX*

 KEY CONTRIBUTIONS ETHICS, POLITICAL PHILOSOPHY

SECOND WAVE

Second-wave feminism is generally considered to have gained **momentum** on the **liberal tides** sweeping **Western countries** in the **1960s**. Increasingly, women recognized that the **freedoms** and **equalities** granted to **earlier generations** merely **redressed selected issues**, and that women still existed in the **strait-jacket of male-defined stereotypes** – **wife**, **mother**, **sex object** – reinforced by **media**, **family**, **religion**, and other **social forces**.

THE OTHER

The groundwork for this second wave had been laid by the ideas of French existentialist philosopher **Simone de Beauvoir**, whose 1949 book, ***The Second Sex***, argued that women had historically been defined as "**other**", allocated a **secondary** and **supporting role** that **allowed the male sex to define itself** in what it perceived as **positive "primary" terms**. Man is **active**, goes out to **work**, is **physically strong**, **rational,** etc.; woman is **passive**, **stays at home**, is **physically weaker**, **emotional**.

FEMALE ROLES

Key to de Beauvoir's critique of these **traditional roles** is the **existentialist assertion** that **we have no "core" self**, but are **completely free to define ourselves by our actions** – and so, as she famously observed, "**one is not born, but rather becomes a woman**". This also suggests a **reason for why more women don't simply rise up** and **discard these false identities**. As noted previously, existentialists argue that our **complete freedom creates** *anxiety*, making us turn to **comforting beliefs** and **excuses** that **shield us from such frightening responsibility**. Traditional female roles **persist**, then, because, de Beauvoir argues, **although they reinforce inequality**, for **some women at least** they **provide partial refuge** from the **anguish of facing their own limitless freedom**.

THE DEMIURGE

One response to the problem of evil is that the material world was not in fact created by God, but by a less competent, less benevolent, or possibly even malignant entity.

 NAME SIMONE WEIL

 DATES 1909–43

 NATIONALITY FRENCH

 SCHOOL CHRISTIAN SOCIALISM

 MAIN WORKS *GRAVITY AND GRACE; WAITING ON GOD*

 KEY CONTRIBUTIONS PHILOSOPHY OF RELIGION

THE CRAFTSMAN

The idea of the **demiurge** first appears in **Plato's** *Timaeus*, where the **creator** of the **physical world** is pictured as a **lesser but still benign creator deity** (from the Greek *demiurgos*, "craftsman").

GNOSTICISM

From here, this entity evolved through **Neoplatonism** (discussed previously) and **Gnosticism** (an **early variant form of Christianity**), along the way acquiring a reputation for **ineptitude**, **ignorance**, and even **malevolence**, to the point where the **Cathars** (a **medieval Christian sect**) **equated this figure** with **Satan** himself.

DUALISM

In this **opposition** of **spirit** and **matter**, Gnosticism comes close to the **dualism** found in such religions as **Manichaeism** and **Zoroastrianism**, both of which proposed the **existence of two equally powerful but antithetical warring forces**. Whatever the case, Gnosticism argued that we are essentially **spiritual beings trapped in a material prison**, the **only escape** from which was to **reject** the **illusions of physical reality** and **cultivate our spark of innate divinity**.

GRAVITY AND GRACE

In **modern theology**, the view persists arguably in the **religious philosophy** of French Christian philosopher **Simone Weil**. While she **did not explicitly identify with this tradition** (though she did **praise** the **Cathars**), she nonetheless pictured the **physical world as completely divorced from God**, a realm of **suffering, pain, selfishness, baseness**, and **injustice** that merely **serves to remind us** of **what we are not**, **stimulating us** to **strive for connection** with **that which we truly are**. **Consciously accepting** the "**gravity**" of these **forces**, we may **experience God's "grace"**.

FALSIFICATION

Responding to logical positivism, Karl Popper argued that what advanced scientific knowledge was not positive proof, but negative evidence – proof that a theory was false.

 NAME KARL POPPER

 DATES 1902–94

 NATIONALITY AUSTRIAN

 SCHOOL ANALYTIC PHILOSOPHY

 MAIN WORKS *THE LOGIC OF SCIENTIFIC DISCOVERY; THE OPEN SOCIETY AND ITS ENEMIES*

 KEY CONTRIBUTIONS EPISTEMOLOGY, POLITICAL PHILOSOPHY, PHILOSOPHY OF SCIENCE

THE PROBLEM OF INDUCTION

Logical positivists such as **A. J. Ayer** had argued that the **only meaningful statements** were those that were **logically undeniable** or else **verifiable through experience**. However, viewed in this way, because of the **problem of induction**, it seems **difficult to imagine any conclusive proof** to back up **statements of scientific fact**.

FALSE THEORIES

Popper's insight was to realize that **false scientific theories** could in fact teach us as much as "**true**" ones, and that **theories could only ever be accepted provisionally**. **Aristotle's notion of gravity** held sway until **Newton's theories** supplanted them, which were then held as "**true**" until Einstein revised them; in turn, Einstein's **may one day be overturned** by fresh ones. **Science** therefore **advances not by proving theories**, but by **falsifying them**, to **replace them with better ones**.

PSEUDOSCIENCE

For Popper, what made a theory "**scientific**" was therefore its **testability**. Could it (conceivably) be **falsified**? What **future evidence** or **insight** might **overturn it**? If none, then it **wasn't scientific** at all – such as (Popper argued) **astrology**, or the **theories of Marx** and **Freud** – and should be classed as "**pseudoscience**". Of course, this didn't mean that such theories were **meaningless**, merely that they did not advance **scientific knowledge**.

EMOTIVISM

Another consequence of logical positivism is that ethical statements were reduced to the status of irrational sentiments.

 NAME R. M. HARE

 DATES 1919–2002

 NATIONALITY ENGLISH

 SCHOOL ANALYTIC PHILOSOPHY

 MAIN WORKS *THE LANGUAGE OF MORALS; MORAL THINKING*

 KEY CONTRIBUTIONS ETHICS

BOO–HURRAH

Ayer's assertion that **meaningful statements** were either **logical tautologies** or **must be subject to empirical proof** effectively **relegated ethics** to **emotional expressions**. "**Murder is wrong**" simply means "**I hate murder**", an **emotional value judgement**. But such **preferences**, like your partisan support of your local football team, aren't something you can have a **rational debate** about. For which reason this is known as the **"boo–hurrah" theory of ethics**.

META-ETHICS

For obvious reasons, **many philosophers** were **concerned about this move**. This is really a debate about **what sort of thing ethics is** – a field called *meta-ethics*. Thinkers such as **Kant** argued that **moral statements** should be *universalizable*. If I say "*Stealing is unethical*" then it's implied that this **should be true for everyone**, not only for **myself**. But **emotional responses**, just like **taste in food or wine**, are not **objective**, **universal propositions**, but **personal**, **subjective expressions** that are likely to be **different for different people** (and not therefore **universally true for everyone**).

UNIVERSAL PRESCRIPTIVISM

While he agreed with **Ayer** that **moral statements** are **not about facts**, English philosopher **R. M. Hare** argued that we can still have a **rational debate about ethics**. This is because in holding such views as "**Stealing is unethical**", I am **not just expressing a personal preference** (as with **supporting a football team**). My **preference implies actions** for **myself** and **others**: not only **won't I steal**, but I **want to live in a world where I'm not stolen from**. In this way, **moral statements** can still be **universalizable**. This approach formed the basis for Hare's *preference utilitarianism*, which, instead of **pleasure**, sought to **maximize** a person's **preferences** or personal **interests**.

ARTIFICIAL INTELLIGENCE

Mathematician Alan Turing proposed that, in order for it to be considered intelligent, it should be sufficient for a machine to fool someone into thinking that it was human.

 NAME ALAN TURING

 DATES 1912–54

 NATIONALITY ENGLISH

 SCHOOL BEHAVIOURISM

 MAIN WORKS "COMPUTING MACHINERY AND INTELLIGENCE"

 KEY CONTRIBUTIONS PHILOSOPHY OF MIND

THINKING MACHINES

Today's **computers** can **perform calculations quicker than humans**, or ones we're **not even capable of**, and this is a boundary that is being **pushed back further every day**. But is this **apparently intelligent behaviour** "thinking", or just a **superficial imitation** of human thought?

THE TURING TEST

To settle this question, mathematician **Alan Turing** (who helped break the **Nazi secret codes** in the **Second World War**) argued that to be **considered intelligent**, a machine need only *pass for* human. The **Turing Test** (as it's become known) involves **two humans** and a **computer**, all **hidden** from one another. One human passes **written questions** to the other two

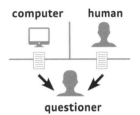

participants, who **respond in kind**. After a certain time, the questioner decides **which participant is human**. If a machine can **pass this test**, Turing argues, then surely we must consider it to be "**thinking**".

OBJECTIONS

This **thought experiment** has caused much **controversy**, and **numerous objections** have been raised. First of all, Turing's approach owes much to *behaviourism*, and the idea that it is **observable behaviour** (in this case, **written communication**) that counts. No matter what is going on "**inside**" the computer, it's what's going on "outside" that counts. As a result, some philosophers – such as **John Searle** (see later) – concede that this might be considered "**thinking**" in a **limited sense**, but argue that it is **insufficient** for "**consciousness**". Others, however, such as physicist **Roger Penrose**, argue that there are **certain forms of thinking** that will forever remain **beyond the grasp of machines**.

For instance, Penrose argues, a human can see that A x B is the same as B x A, whatever the values of A and B.

> If A = 3 and B = 4, then
> AxB=12, and BxA=12.
>
> If A=2 and B=4, then
> AxB=8, and BxA=8.
>
> If A=4 and B=4, then
> AxB=16, and BxA=16.

But a machine cannot achieve such an insight. It must either calculate every possible value of A and B (an infinite task), or else it must be programmed in as a general rule. And there may be infinitely many such rules...

THE ABSURD

Driven to seek meaning in a meaningless world, our only recourse, Camus argued, is to live a life of rebellion.

  NAME ALBERT CAMUS

 DATES 1913–60

NATIONALITY FRENCH ALGERIAN

 SCHOOL EXISTENTIALISM

 MAIN WORKS *THE OUTSIDER; THE PLAGUE; THE MYTH OF SISYPHUS; THE REBEL*

 KEY CONTRIBUTIONS ETHICS

CONTEMPORARY PHILOSOPHY

THE MYTH OF SISYPHUS

Like **Sisyphus** – the king from Greek mythology condemned by the gods eternally **to roll a boulder up a hill**, only for it to **roll back down before reaching the top** – **our existence is inherently meaningless**. And yet, as human beings we seem **unavoidably driven to seek meaning**. It is this **contradiction** that gives existence an *absurd* quality.

THE OUTSIDER

Like other **existentialists**, **Camus** also expressed some of his ideas in **fictional form**. His most famous novel, ***The Outsider***, describes the life of **Meursault**, an **apparently average man** who nonetheless finds himself **at odds with the world**. His **mother dies**, but he finds himself **unable to shed a tear at her funeral**; caught up in events he **doesn't understand**, he ends up **shooting someone**, but at his own trial **can offer no defence or motive**. Like the protagonists in **Franz Kafka's novels**, Meursault is an **outsider**, alone in his apparent recognition of **life's meaningless absurdity**.

REVOLT

How, then, are we to face this absurdity? We **cannot simply accept it**, because the two things – our **desire for meaning**, and the **meaninglessness of existence** – are **ultimately irreconcilable**, which also rules out the **hope that our life will improve**. A life devoted to **pleasure** or **forgetful oblivion**, even **dedication to some cause**, would merely represent a **forlorn attempt at escape**. The only answer, then, is **rebellion**: to **deny our fate** by living a **full, conscious life** *despite* its meaninglessness.

LIBERTY

Isaiah Berlin argued that liberty, or political freedom, had evolved through history into two separate traditions.

 NAME ISAIAH BERLIN

 DATES 1909–97

 NATIONALITY BRITISH (LATVIAN BORN)

 SCHOOL ANALYTIC PHILOSOPHY

 MAIN WORKS *FOUR ESSAYS ON LIBERTY*

 KEY CONTRIBUTIONS POLITICAL PHILOSOPHY, ETHICS

TWO CONCEPTS OF LIBERTY

Berlin notes that, while **liberty *can* be seen** as a **unified idea possessing two aspects**, philosophers differ as to **which aspect is most important**. **Aristotle** or **Marx** emphasized the **role of the citizen in society**, and the **rights and obligations they possess**. Thinkers such as **Hume**, **Locke**, and **Mill**, however, saw that the **essence of liberty** is **lack of state interference**.

NEGATIVE LIBERTY

In response to these **oppressive aspects** of **positive freedom**, **negative libertarians** argue that individuals must be **free to pursue their own ends**. As **Mill** says, if you want to **eat or drink too much – unless it affects others** – how is that **society's concern**? Such a view is at the root of modern ***free market economics*** and ***neoliberalism***, which claim that **society benefits most** from **minimal state involvement**, allowing **individuals** and **companies** to **succeed** or **fail** as **merit dictates**. However, this **assumes that everyone starts on an equal playing field**, and those who **fail earn their deserts**. But is this true?

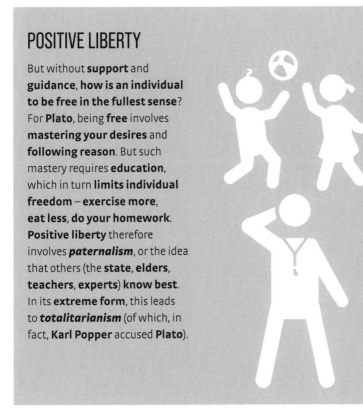

POSITIVE LIBERTY

But without **support** and **guidance, how is an individual to be free in the fullest sense**? For **Plato**, being **free** involves **mastering your desires** and **following reason**. But such mastery requires **education**, which in turn **limits individual freedom – exercise more, eat less, do your homework**. **Positive liberty** therefore involves ***paternalism***, or the idea that others (the **state, elders, teachers, experts) know best**. In its **extreme form**, this leads to ***totalitarianism*** (of which, in fact, **Karl Popper** accused **Plato**).

IDENTITY THEORY

Mind–Brain Identity Theory attempts to resolve the mind–body problem by claiming that there is in fact no problem, because mind and brain are identical.

 NAME DAVID ARMSTRONG

 DATES 1926–2014

 NATIONALITY AUSTRALIAN

 SCHOOL ANALYTIC PHILOSOPHY

 MAIN WORKS *A MATERIALIST THEORY OF MIND*

 KEY CONTRIBUTIONS PHILOSOPHY OF MIND, METAPHYSICS

PHYSICALISM

Mind–Brain Identity Theory originated with philosophers **Ullin Place** and **J. J. C. Smart** in the 1950s, but was most fully developed by **David Armstrong**. It is the general belief that **mental events *are*** simply **physical brain events**. This may sound obvious to anyone who **rejects religious** or **spiritual accounts** of **human nature**, but even for ***physicalists***, the assertion that **mind *is* brain** actually throws up a number of **tricky problems**.

DIFFERENT DESCRIPTIONS

For a start, **mental** and **physical descriptions** have **different meanings**. "I am happy" doesn't mean the same as "**these neurons in my brain are active**". However, **identity theorists** can argue that this is simply a **quirk of language** given our **current scientific knowledge**: "**this water is freezing**" doesn't literally mean the same as "**these molecular bonds are forming**", but the **meaning of the first** *can be **reduced*** to the **second**, just as – when we **fully understand the brain** – "**I'm happy**" will be **reducible** to "**this group of neurons is active**".

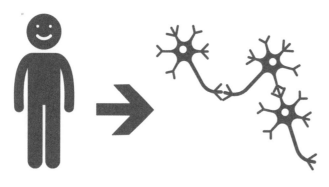

TYPES AND TOKENS

However, another issue concerns **how physical and mental events correspond**. Do **all *types*** of **brain states** correspond with ***types*** of **mental event**? Does "angry" always **light up the same group of neurons** in **all people**? Or might **each instance (*token*)** of my **anger** have a **different neurological basis** to **yours**, or even to **previous instances** (*tokens*) of my **own anger**? If so, while there is obviously some **close relationship** between **mind** and **brain**, it seems **more complicated than identity theory proposes**.

HERMENEUTICS

*The field of philosophical hermeneutics encompasses the range of issues
we face in attempting any form of interpretation.*

 NAME HANS-GEORG GADAMER

 DATES 1900–2002

 NATIONALITY GERMAN

 SCHOOL HERMENEUTICS

 MAIN WORKS *TRUTH AND METHOD*

 KEY CONTRIBUTIONS METAPHYSICS, EPISTEMOLOGY,
AESTHETICS

BIBLE STUDIES

Hermeneutics is the **theory of interpretation**. It grew from nineteenth-century **biblical studies**, where it was realized that **deeper understanding of scripture** required recognizing the **cultural** and **historical context** in which **texts were written**. German philosopher **Wilhelm Dilthey** (1833–1911) **expanded hermeneutics** to **include all human sciences involving textual interpretation**.

THE HERMENEUTIC CIRCLE

A key concept here is the "**hermeneutic circle**". The **meaning** of **individual concepts** and sentences within a **text** is **coloured** by **understanding** of their **general cultural** and **historical context**. However, our understanding of **sentences** and **concepts informs** and **changes** our understanding of the **context**. **Parts** and **whole** are interrelated, and **any process of interpretation must therefore be circular**.

SITUATEDNESS

Modern or *philosophical* hermeneutics is associated with German philosopher **Hans-Georg Gadamer**, a student of **Heidegger** whose *Being and Time* was **itself a hermeneutic attempt** to "**interpret**" existence within the **context of a being** that **finds itself already "situated"** in the world, and where the **attempt to interpret existence** is **pre-shaped** by the **nature of existence itself**.

HORIZONS

Applying this lesson, Gadamer focuses on **language**, which he sees as **mediating all knowledge** of the **world**. As such, **growing up** within a **culture** or **tradition** also **traps us within it** – we are **bounded by our own cultural "horizon"** – and any attempt to use **linguistic** and **conceptual tools** to **interpret other cultures** is always **shaped by our own often unconscious attitudes** and **beliefs**. This makes neutral or objective **interpretation impossible**, and **any act of interpretation** must therefore **always be** a **dialogue** or **synthesis** – a "**fusion of horizons**" – that **creates something new**.

SITUATIONISM

Situationism saw modern capitalist society as replacing authentic social life with a representation or "spectacle" that served consumerism and fostered alienation.

 NAME GUY DEBORD

 DATES 1931–94

 NATIONALITY FRENCH

 SCHOOL CONTINENTAL PHILOSOPHY (SITUATIONISM)

 MAIN WORKS *THE SOCIETY OF THE SPECTACLE*

 KEY CONTRIBUTIONS POLITICAL PHILOSOPHY, SOCIAL THEORY

COMMODIFICATION

Originated by French **Marxist** and **anarchist** philosopher **Guy Debord**, **Situationist International** was a **radical artistic** and **political movement** that provided a **critique of modern capitalist society**, arguing that it turned the **features of everyday life** into "**commodities**", fostering **false desires** for **products** and **experiences** that can be **owned** and **consumed**.

THE SPECTACLE

Capitalism transforms life into a "**spectacle**", where **traditional human relations** are **replaced** by their **representation**. Thus, through **advertising**, **mass media**, and **popular culture**, **consumerist society** created a "**spectacle**" **reflecting** and **reinforcing class distinctions**, making us **see other people** through the **lens of their material status**.

THE DRUGGED SPECTATOR

The **goal** of **Situationism** was therefore to "**wake up**" the **drugged spectator** from the **spectacle imposed** by **modern consumerist society**, which it did through various means. *Détournement*, or what is now called *adbusting*, involved **vandalizing billboards** and **hoardings** in order to **subvert their message**. *Dérive* was the practice of **wandering around** or **occupying public spaces** for purposes **other than commercial interests intended** them, and attempted **to create in the participant** a **more authentic emotional** and **intellectual experience** – a *situation*.

REVOLUTION

The **ultimate goal** of all this was **revolution** – which the **movement almost achieved**, providing a driving force behind the **turbulent events** of **May 1968** in **Paris**, where **demonstrators** almost **brought down de Gaulle's government**. Part of the reason the movement **failed to achieve this** is perhaps that Situationism (a **term that Debord himself rejected**) itself became **commodified**, becoming **just another "ism"** to be written about in books...

KNOWLEDGE

Plato's definition of knowledge held sway for over two millennia, until Edmund Gettier highlighted in it a significant flaw.

 NAME EDMUND GETTIER

 DATES 1927–

 NATIONALITY AMERICAN

 SCHOOL ANALYTIC PHILOSOPHY

 MAIN WORKS "IS JUSTIFIED TRUE BELIEF KNOWLEDGE?"

 KEY CONTRIBUTIONS EPISTEMOLOGY

THE TRIPARTITE DEFINITION

In his ***Theaetetus***, **Plato** advanced the idea that **knowledge required three elements**: it must be **consciously held** or **expressed**, rest on **sufficient justification**, and be true. We **can't know something** that's **false**, that we've **no evidence for**, or that has **never occurred to us**.

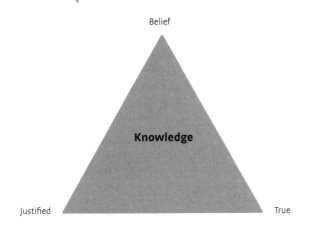

Belief

Knowledge

Justified   True

FALSE BELIEFS

The problem with this is that you seem to hold a **true, justified belief** ("The **successful candidate will wear a gold watch**"), that most of us would hesitate to term "**knowledge**". But why? You may say that your belief that Jim would get the job was **false** – but then **Plato doesn't require your knowledge not to be inferred from false supporting beliefs**. Nor does it matter that **your gold watch information related to Jim**, and was merely **coincidentally true for Tim**. It only matters that it *was* true and **you had justification for it** (your "**usually trustworthy source**"). Hmm. Was **Plato wrong**?

GETTIER PROBLEMS

Edmund Gettier challenged this view with **examples** that seemed to meet **Plato's criteria**, but that nonetheless we **wouldn't class as knowledge**. For instance (**simplifying** and **adapting Gettier's example**), suppose that **Jim and Tim apply for a job** where you work. You hear **two bits of gossip** from a usually **trustworthy source**: Jim will get the job; the **successful candidate wears a gold watch**. As a result, you believe that, "**the person who gets the job will be wearing a gold watch**". However, the **gossip is wrong** (partly): **Tim gets the job** – but, it turns out, previously **unknown to you**, he is also wearing a gold watch.

Tim   Jim

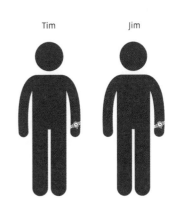

DEATH OF THE AUTHOR

While traditional literary criticism saw the author's intentions as key to the meaning of his text, Roland Barthes argued that these were actually irrelevant.

 NAME ROLAND BARTHES

 DATES 1915–80

 NATIONALITY FRENCH

 SCHOOL STRUCTURALISM

 MAIN WORKS *'THE DEATH OF THE AUTHOR'*; *MYTHOLOGIES*; *THE PLEASURE OF THE TEXT*

 KEY CONTRIBUTIONS AESTHETICS, SOCIAL THEORY

THE AUTHOR-GOD

Barthes argued that when we **aim to provide** a **definitive interpretation** of a **literary text** based on what the **author apparently intended**, we make a number of **unwarranted assumptions**. First, we **assume** that we can actually **find out these intentions**. But **can we really say** with any **certainty**, for example, what **Balzac** or some other writer **meant by a particular line**? And, of course, this **presumes** that the **author in question** actually *had* a **definite intention in mind**. This approach, Barthes argues, therefore **treats the author** as a **form of deity**, delivering His message from **on high**, and **literary criticism** itself becomes almost a form of **theology**.

THE SCRIPTOR

In proposing the **death of the author**, Barthes is **not only rejecting this picture** of textual interpretation (what has been called **"the intentional fallacy"**), but also **reacting against the idea** that a **text can have one "authoritative" meaning** (pun intended). In contrast, Barthes argues that a text is **composed of many levels of meaning**, and **multiple forces** are **involved** in its **production** (**social, cultural, historical, psychological**, etc.). As such, an author is merely a *scriptor*, a **means of transmitting these forces**.

MULTIPLE MEANINGS

In addition to this, **each reader elicits his or her own subjective meaning** from a text, and **each reading** is in effect the **creation of a new text**, a new perspective. Given all of this, **on what basis are we to privilege *one single* interpretation**?

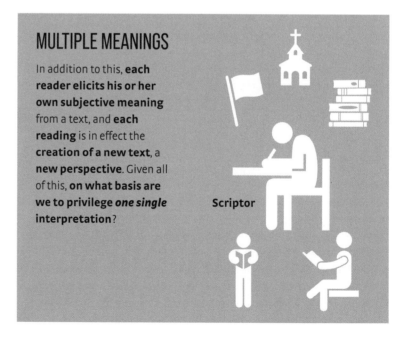

Scriptor

THE BRAIN IN A VAT

The sceptical argument that there is no way of knowing what is real was updated into technological terms by the thought experiment of the brain in a vat.

 NAME HILARY PUTNAM

 DATES 1926–2016

 NATIONALITY AMERICAN

 SCHOOL ANALYTIC PHILOSOPHY

 MAIN WORKS *'BRAINS IN A VAT'; MEANING AND REFERENCE; REPRESENTATION AND REALITY; MIND, LANGUAGE AND REALITY*

 KEY CONTRIBUTIONS METAPHYSICS, EPISTEMOLOGY, PHILOSOPHY OF MIND

SOLIPSISM

From **Zhuang Zi** to **Descartes** and beyond, philosophers have considered the **problem of how we might tell whether the world we perceive exists objectively**, or whether it is some form of **illusion**, existing **only for me (solipsism)**. This **seems** like a **far-fetched possibility**, but **logically** there is actually **great difficulty** in **ruling out such an illusion**.

Brain in a vat

TECHNOLOGICAL DECEPTION

Rather than frame this idea in terms of **dreaming** or **deception** by **evil demons** (as **Descartes** did), American philosopher **Gilbert Harman** (b.1938) asked us to **imagine** that we were **disembodied brains** kept in a **vat of chemicals**, **wired up to a computer** that supplied **electrical signals** to the **brain**, convincing us we're **experiencing reality**, when actually it's a **simulated illusion** (as in *The Matrix*). **Could we spot the deception**? Might it be true that you're now **living in such a condition**, and **don't know it**?

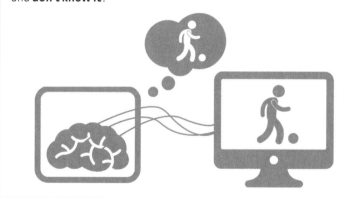

CAUSAL REFERENCE

Hilary Putnam argued that there was indeed a way of **defeating this type of scepticism**. If I think, "**I'm a brain in a vat**", for this statement to be true, the words "**brain**" and "**vat**" must **refer to** (and be **caused by**) actual **brains and vats**. But if I am a brain in a vat, then the words that **I've learnt to refer to these things** do not relate to **actual brains and vats**, but have come into being in relation to **false simulations** of these objects. And so, **because of the way language works**, it **must be false** that I'm a brain in a vat.

FUNCTIONALISM

Developing the behaviourist approach to the mind, Functionalism argued that the mind is no more than a system of inputs and outputs.

THE BLACK BOX

Because of problems with **behaviourism**, certain philosophers advocated for a **more complex theory** that didn't see the **mind** just in terms of **potential** or **actual behaviour**, but rather in terms of an **information-processing system**, like a **computer**. Things were **fed in**, and things **came out**. As with behaviourism, however, it **didn't really matter what went on "inside" this machine**, which for all intents and purposes could be considered an inscrutable "**black box**". All that mattered was how the machine *functioned*.

PROBLEMS

While **functionalism** is still a **popular view**, there are **well-known problems** with it, and **Putnam** himself later **criticized** it. Not least of these is the idea that **mental reality cannot simply be conceived of in terms of function** – that there are **things that go on** inside the black box that ***aren't*** **merely functional**.

MULTIPLE REALIZABILITY

An interesting **consequence** of this view – first introduced by **Hilary Putnam** – is *multiple realizability*. This is simply the notion that, **if a mind is simply a collection of inputs and outputs** that **function as a processing system**, it **doesn't really matter what these parts are made of** – **biological cells**, **microchips**, or whatever. We see this notion, for instance, in ***Star Trek*** and other **sci-fi**, where the crew encounter "**non-carbon-based life-forms**", implying that "**life**" is **capable of being realized in multiple ways**.

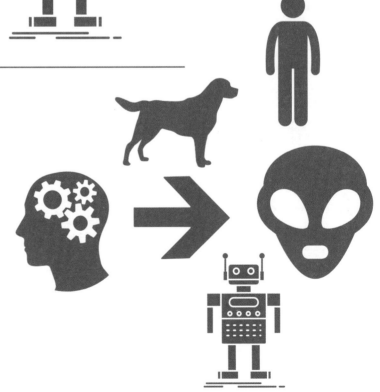

THE VEIL OF IGNORANCE

John Rawls argued that a truly just society can only be achieved when those who frame its rules do so without regard to their own personal characteristics and inherent biases.

 NAME JOHN RAWLS

 DATES 1921–2002

 NATIONALITY AMERICAN

 SCHOOL ANALYTIC PHILOSOPHY

 MAIN WORKS *A THEORY OF JUSTICE*

 KEY CONTRIBUTIONS ETHICS, POLITICAL PHILOSOPHY

BACKGROUND BIAS

However, no matter how **wise**, **experienced**, and **proficient** these **leaders**, they still embody certain **characteristics**, **values**, and **attitudes** – from their **upbringing**, **religion**, **gender**, **race**, **economic background**, and so forth. So, no matter how **well meaning**, such characteristics **influence our decisions** in often **unconscious ways**, providing **bias**.

PHILOSOPHER KINGS

A society's **rules** and **laws** are often left in the hands of its **elders**: the **wise** and **learned**, those who have benefited from **experience**, or have risen to the **top of their professions**. As **Plato** argued, in order to **create a society** that will embody **principles of justice and fairness**, its **rulers** (his ***philosopher kings***) should **embody the best** in all senses.

VEIL OF IGNORANCE ← rules

THE ORIGINAL POSITION

To avoid this, **Rawls** asked us to **imagine society's laws** as created by **individuals who possess no such characteristics**. They exist, in his phrase, ***behind a veil of ignorance***, from which they choose how **everyone** – regardless of individual **characteristics** – **should be treated**. Like **Hobbes's *state of nature***, this ***original position*** is **not a practical solution** but a hypothetical scenario intended to highlight what **justice should look like**. As a **legislator**, the **laws** I create **must apply** whether I'm **black or white**, **male or female**, **gay or straight**, or any of the other things that might define me. Would Plato's kings be so keen on his **republic** if there was a chance they might be a **worker drone**? It's only through such "**ignorance**" that we can create a **truly fair and just society**.

PARADIGM SHIFTS

Thomas Kuhn argued against the view that science advanced gradually by verifying or falsifying hypotheses, proposing instead that it shifted dramatically between different paradigms.

 NAME THOMAS KUHN

 DATES 1922–96

 NATIONALITY AMERICAN

 SCHOOL ANALYTIC PHILOSOPHY

 MAIN WORKS *THE STRUCTURE OF SCIENTIFIC REVOLUTIONS*

 KEY CONTRIBUTIONS EPISTEMOLOGY

INCOMMENSURABILITY

Kuhn illustrates his point using the **shift** between the **Ptolemaic contention** that the **Earth** was the **centre of the universe** (*geocentrism*) to the **Copernican assertion** that the **Earth orbits the Sun** (*heliocentrism*). These two *paradigms*, he argued, were **so different**, and the **principles** that **underpinned** them so **at odds**, as to represent **completely** *incommensurable* worldviews. It was almost as if they were **speaking different languages** where **translation** between them was **not completely possible**.

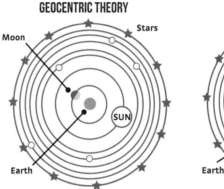
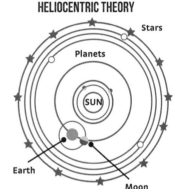

GEOCENTRIC THEORY

Stars
Moon
SUN
Earth

HELIOCENTRIC THEORY

Stars
Planets
SUN
Earth
Moon

ANOMALIES

What, then, causes the **shift** between **one paradigm** and **another**? It's easy in **hindsight** to assume that **heliocentrism** was simply more "**rational**" and provided a "**better**" **explanation of events**. It was true that the **Ptolemaic system** had become more **complicated** and **unwieldy**, creating more and more *anomalies* as more **information on planetary movements** was **amassed**. But **this did not make it "wrong"**, necessarily – the **universe might just be very complicated** in that way. Rather, Kuhn argues, the **increasing anomalies** made certain scientists **lose faith** in the **Ptolemaic system's ability** to **solve scientific problems**.

PUZZLE SOLVING

When a paradigm is **broadly accepted**, it allows scientists to **concentrate** on what Kuhn calls "**normal science**". This is the **everyday research** that **applies** the **grand theory** to **small-scale problems** and **puzzles**, and that **facilitates technological progress**. It is only when a system can **no longer provide this framework** – when it **throws up too many anomalies** – that it **ceases to be useful**, and it becomes tempting to **abandon it** for **another system** that promises **greater scope** to **solve new problems**.

POWER AND SURVEILLANCE

Michel Foucault argued that members of society are shaped and controlled by the values and power relations inherent in social institutions and the language these employ.

 NAME MICHEL FOUCAULT

 DATES 1926–84

 NATIONALITY FRENCH

SCHOOL CONTINENTAL PHILOSOPHY (POST-STRUCTURALISM)

MAIN WORKS *MADNESS AND CIVILISATION; DISCIPLINE AND PUNISH; THE HISTORY OF SEXUALITY*

KEY CONTRIBUTIONS POLITICAL PHILOSOPHY, SOCIAL THEORY

THE GREAT CONFINEMENT

In his early work on **madness**, Foucault argues that **"insanity"** is **not a natural concept**, but one **constructed by social forces**. During the so-called **Age of Reason** spanning the seventeenth to nineteenth centuries, "the **Great Confinement**" **labelled** and **incarcerated** individuals who displayed various forms of **deviant behaviour**, thus creating a **class** of **"mental illness"** that reflected the **new, stricter criteria** of **rationality** and **sanity**.

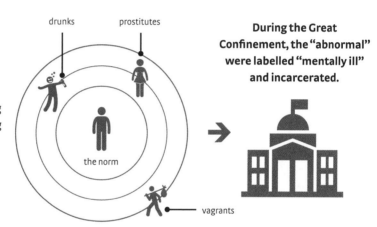

During the Great Confinement, the "abnormal" were labelled "mentally ill" and incarcerated.

drunks — prostitutes — the norm — vagrants

WILL TO POWER

This is **not necessarily to say** that **"madness"** or **"mental illness" does not exist**, but merely that these are concepts whose **meaning** and **application** are **socially constructed**, and therefore *neither objective nor fixed*. Influenced by **Nietzsche's concept** of ***will to power***, Foucault attempted to show how such **concepts** and **perspectives reflect the values of those in power**.

PANOPTICON

The intriguing thing about Foucault's theory is that **political** and **social power** is **not wielded openly**, but **"buried"** within the **political**, **scientific**, and **cultural structures** that **make up society**. In a later work on **criminality**, Foucault utilizes as a **metaphor** for this **type of control** Jeremy Bentham's ***Panopticon***, an **"ideal" prison** where the **inmates** are **monitored** by a **central guard tower**. However, this **"monitoring"** is **not effected directly** but in such a way that, because the **guard** is **hidden**, the **inmates never know when they are/aren't being watched**. In a similar way, Foucault implies, the **structures of power do not always employ direct means**, but rather **encourage us** to **"monitor"** and **police ourselves**, as we **internalize** the **values** and **concepts** we are **taught to employ** in order **to function in society**.

SEX

Foucault disputed the traditionally accepted "repressive hypothesis", arguing that sexuality was not so much "repressed" as "created" and shaped by a rise in sexual discourse.

THE REPRESSIVE HYPOTHESIS

Philosophers such as **Herbert Marcuse** (discussed earlier) argued that **sexual repression** arose **in conjunction with capitalism**, requiring the creation of **pliable workers** and **consumers** whose **sexuality** could be **channelled for commercial ends**, a **constraint** that has only somewhat **eased in recent times**.

CONFESSIONAL

In contrast, **Foucault** pointed out that the **alleged rise** of **sexual repression** actually **coincided** with the **growth** of the **scientific study of sex**. In this sense, while we often think of the **Victorian era** as a **repressive period** where sex was a **taboo topic**, it actually involved an **increase in attention** to **sexual matters** paid by **doctors**, **educators**, and **legislators**. These professions were themselves merely **secular equivalents** of the **priest** to whom the **penitent** is **forced to confess** the most **intimate details** of his life.

SEXUAL NORMALITY

Foucault's view is **opposed** (for instance) by **conservative philosophers** such as **Roger Scruton** (1944–2020), who considered there to be a **"normal"** or **"morally acceptable" form of sexuality**, and that such things as **homosexuality**, even some forms of **masturbation**, are **perversions**, reflecting a **narcissistic failure** truly to **engage with the "other"** (which he sees as characteristic of **mature sexuality**). And whereas Foucault sees **gender** and **sexual identity** as products of **social forces**, Scruton views them as **biological determinations**.

CONSTRUCTED SEXUALITY

Foucault is therefore arguing that, during this period, **medicine**, **education**, and **law** are actually **creating** and **moulding "sexuality"** (much as it did with **madness** and **criminality**). As such, for Foucault, **sexual behaviour** and **"preference"** are **not inherent properties** of an **individual**, **determined** perhaps by **biology**, but **socially constructed**, taking **different forms** in **different cultures** and **periods**.

ABORTION

Judith Jarvis Thomson argues that, even if a foetus has an inherent right to life, this will mostly be superseded by a woman's rights over her own body.

 NAME JUDITH JARVIS THOMSON

 DATES 1929–

 NATIONALITY AMERICAN

 SCHOOL ANALYTIC PHILOSOPHY

 MAIN WORKS "A DEFENSE OF ABORTION"

 KEY CONTRIBUTIONS ETHICS, METAPHYSICS

THE FAMOUS VIOLINIST

You wake up in a hospital bed, joined by various tubes to a famous violinist, who is, **without consent**, using your kidneys (his have failed, and you share a super-rare blood type). Would you feel **violated** or **outraged**? Would you disconnect him immediately, even though **he'll die**? But it's *your* body! That **same justification** would **permit abortion**.

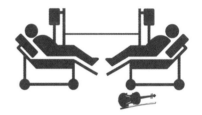

THE GROWING CHILD

You are **stuck in your house** with a **rapidly growing child** (think *Alice in Wonderland*). It will eventually **crush you**. Would you be entitled to **call on someone else to stop this**, even if it results in the **child's death**? Here, the **house** is the **woman's body**, and **external help** would be **medical abortion**. Again, **Thomson** argues, **access to abortion** is an **extension of a woman's rights over her own body** (she *owns* the house).

PEOPLE-SEEDS

Finally, there are **"people-seeds"** floating around the air, which **grow into persons** if they **get into your house**. Those who want this **open their windows**; those who don't, **close them** or put a **mesh over their windows** to enjoy fresh air. If a person-seed nonetheless gets through a mesh, should the house-owner be **denied the right** to remove it? As for people-seeds and meshes, so for **foetuses** and **contraception. Consent to sex** (open windows) is **not consent to pregnancy**. As these three thought experiments suggest, for all except **trivial reasons**, Thomson argues, a woman should have a **right to abortion**.

RELIGIOUS LANGUAGE

Antony Flew combined the evidence-based approach of logical positivism with the falsificationism of Karl Popper to argue that religious language and belief was largely meaningless.

 NAME ANTONY FLEW

 DATES 1923–2010

 NATIONALITY ENGLISH

 SCHOOL ANALYTIC PHILOSOPHY

 MAIN WORKS *THE PRESUMPTION OF ATHEISM*; "THEOLOGY AND FALSIFICATION"

 KEY CONTRIBUTIONS PHILOSOPHY OF RELIGION

THE INVISIBLE GARDENER

Out walking, you and your friend pass a **plot of land**. Your friend thinks it's a "**garden**", but you point out that it seems **wild** and **untended**. The argument rolls on, but even when you set up **cameras** and **motion detectors** (which **find nothing**), your friend remains **immune to persuasion**, claiming eventually that the **gardener** may be **invisible** and **incorporeal**. Is your friend being **irrational**?

MEANING AND FALSIFICATION

Flew's point here refers to **religious language** and **belief**. If a believer says, "**God loves us**", an **atheist** may point to all the **evil** and **tragedy** the **omnipotent deity** apparently **allows**. Doesn't this disprove his love? The **believer** who remains **steadfast** is like the **advocate** for the **invisible gardener**. But if *no* **evidence is relevant**, then aren't such **religious assertions meaningless**?

NO TRUE SCOTSMAN

A related point is made by **Flew** in his example of "**No True Scotsman**". If someone avers that **Scotsmen do not lie**, but is presented with **evidence to the contrary**, they may still assert that "**no *true* Scotsman" would lie** (suggesting that the individual in question isn't a "true" Scotsman). In both the garden and Scotsman examples, Flew suggests that **meaningful assertions must be capable of being falsified**. But **must we interpret religious language in this way**? Perhaps, rather, it is an **expression of value**, or a **poetic response to life**. And even if it cannot be falsified, this surely doesn't make it *meaningless*, but merely places it with **art**, **ethics**, and other **"non-scientific" concerns**.

DECONSTRUCTION

Deconstruction argues that any attempt to advance a single perspective as "true"
will always result in a partial and self-contradictory account of reality.

 NAME JACQUES DERRIDA

 DATES 1930–2004

 NATIONALITY FRENCH (ALGERIA)

 SCHOOL POSTMODERNISM (DECONSTRUCTION)

 MAIN WORKS *OF GRAMMATOLOGY; WRITING AND DIFFERENCE*

 KEY CONTRIBUTIONS METAPHYSICS, EPISTEMOLOGY, PHILOSOPHY OF LANGUAGE, AESTHETICS

APORIA

A movement associated with **postmodern** philosophers **Jacques Derrida** and **Paul de Man** (1919–83), *deconstruction* may be seen as a **reaction against** the **assumption** that **we can take an authoritative standpoint in relation to any subject. A single account** will always be **partial** and **biased**, containing within it *aporias*, **blind spots** or **points of unresolvable difficulty, bias**, or **contradiction** that its **creator is not aware of.**

SPEECH AND WRITING

The foundation of this is **Derrida's account of language**. In the **Western intellectual tradition**, he notes, **writing** is **often portrayed** as the **poor cousin of speech** – a **copy**, a **mere record**. But, he argues, such a **distinction** is **actually symptomatic** of a **deeper tendency** in Western thought to **divide things into binaries**, always **implying a relationship of superiority.** Thus **Plato** emphasizes *reason* over *desire*; **Descartes** sees *mind*, the **source** of *certainty*, as **separate from** *body*, which is **subject to** *doubt*. Against this, **Derrida attempts to show** that **not only may we not divide up reality into such binary oppositions**, but that **in doing so we distort the nature** of the **thing excluded, devaluing it.**

writing **V**

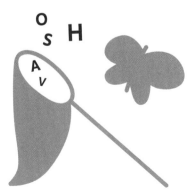

FREE PLAY

But in **denying philosophy authority**, doesn't this **undermine Derrida too**? He disagrees, arguing that he **does not advance his own views**, but **merely "deconstructs" others' viewpoints**, revealing the **"free play" of language** and how, through supplying **different contexts**, **different associations**, the **fixed meanings** that **philosophers attempt to impose** are **undermined** by the **nature of language itself.**

ANTI-REALISM

Anti-realists deny that philosophy aims at a true description of a mind-independent world, providing a mirror to reality.

 NAME RICHARD RORTY

 DATES 1931–2007

 NATIONALITY AMERICA

 SCHOOL NEOPRAGMATISM

 MAIN WORKS *PHILOSOPHY AND THE MIRROR OF NATURE; CONSEQUENCES OF PRAGMATISM; CONTINGENCY, IRONY AND SOLIDARITY*

 KEY CONTRIBUTIONS EPISTEMOLOGY, ETHICS

CORRESPONDENCE

Berkeley's idealism (discussed previously) **opposes** what has been called the ***correspondence theory of truth***, where our **perceptions**, **beliefs**, and **judgements** are **true or not** depending on whether they **correspond to reality**. But if, as Berkeley argued, we can **never get "beyond"** our **own thoughts** and **perceptions**, then we can **never have direct access to a mind-independent reality with which to compare them**.

NEOPRAGMATISM

That said, a **more radical form of anti-realism** has been advanced by American philosopher **Richard Rorty**, who combined **postmodernism** with the **pragmatism** of **C. S. Peirce**. Rorty's ***neopragmatism*** sees **thought** and **language** not as **representations of the world**, but – as Peirce argued – **tools for dealing with it**. And just as **postmodern literary critics deny any authoritative reading of a text**, being subject to **different contexts** and **subjective reactions**, so Rorty argued there **can be no "true" reality independent of multiple possible subjective viewpoints**. If so, then the **viewpoint is "true"** that best works for advancing some particular end.

VARIETIES OF ANTI-REALISM

This conclusion is the **basis of anti-realism**, which can take **many forms**. **Moral anti-realism** may **deny that ethical norms have any real, independent existence outside of social custom**. **Scientific anti-realism** may claim that **science doesn't give us a "true" picture of how the world actually is**, but **merely one** that helps us **predict** and **manipulate** it. Also, although some philosophers take **anti-realism to imply scepticism**, it arguably needn't do so, and **non-sceptical applications of anti-realism** can be found in philosophers as diverse as **Kant** and **Wittgenstein**.

FAITH

Philosophers and theologians have differed as to how they define religious faith, some even arguing that it can be maintained in complete absence of evidence.

 NAME ALVIN PLANTINGA

 DATES 1932–

 NATIONALITY AMERICAN

 SCHOOL ANALYTIC PHILOSOPHY

 MAIN WORKS *GOD AND OTHER MINDS; WARRANTED CHRISTIAN BELIEF*

 KEY CONTRIBUTIONS PHILOSOPHY OF RELIGION

JUSTIFIED BELIEF

As we've seen, **Aquinas** thought that **reason** could play some role in helping a believer to **rationalize faith**; **William James** considered reason to be heavily influenced by **non-rational factors**; while **Pascal** and **Kierkegaard**, to different degrees, viewed faith as **independent of any rational justification**.

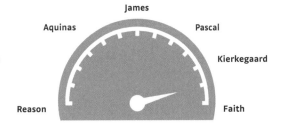

REFORMED EPISTEMOLOGY

A slightly different approach was proposed by **Alvin Plantinga**, who argued that it can be **rational to believe in God** *even if* there is **insufficient evidence or justification**. Utilizing an approach called *reformed epistemology*, Plantinga argues that a belief is *warranted* if our **cognitive faculties** are **functioning properly** (we're not crazy or ill), and that those faculties are suitable for producing **true beliefs** (if we can consider reason to be a reliable guide).

BASIC BELIEFS

While too complex to explore fully here, Plantinga's argument is that if religious beliefs can form part of a **generally reasonable and consistent worldview**, then it shouldn't matter that there is **no conclusive evidence in their favour**. In this sense, such beliefs **may not require external justification**, and may be considered *properly basic* (**fundamental**). A basic belief is something we **rely on but do not prove** – such as our assumption that the **world exists**, and that **we're not dreaming**.

FIDEISM

The problem with this, some argue, is that it would seem to make religious faith **immune to rational argument**, merely **justified by faith alone** (what's called *fideism*). But then, in this sense, would that be any different from our **belief in an external world**?

THE CHINESE ROOM

While many philosophers have sympathy for the computer model of the mind, John Searle argues that computers and brains are fundamentally different.

 NAME JOHN SEARLE

 DATES 1932–

 NATIONALITY AMERICAN

 SCHOOL ANALYTIC PHILOSOPHY

 MAIN WORKS *THE REDISCOVERY OF MIND; THE CONSTRUCTION OF SOCIAL REALITY*

 KEY CONTRIBUTIONS PHILOSOPHY OF MIND, METAPHYSICS

SPEAKING CHINESE

Imagine you are in a **room** with **two hatches at either end**. A **conveyor belt** brings **Chinese symbols** through **one hatch**; you **look these up** in a book, which tells you **which Chinese symbols** to **send out through the other hatch**. Are you **speaking Chinese**?

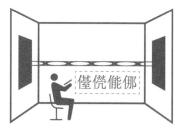

RULES VS MEANING

John Searle – and most people – would **say not**. You would simply be **blindly following rules**. But if this is the case for **human beings**, then what about **computers**? **Artificial intelligence** is driven by *algorithms*, which are simply **sets of instructions**: if *this*, then *that*. They may be very **complicated** and **ingenious** algorithms, but the machine doesn't need to "**understand**" them in order to perform them. In fact, Searle argues, **machines can never "understand"** in this sense. They may "**think**" (in a **weak sense** – what's called *Weak AI*), but not in the **fullest**, **conscious** sense (*Strong AI*). But why?

QUALIA AND INTENTIONALITY

Two **key differences** between **artificial** and **human intelligence** are *qualia* and *intentionality* (discussed elsewhere), the latter of which is most relevant here. When I **say** or **think** something, there is a **certain intention** or **meaning** behind it. This is what makes my "**Chinese speaking**" a **mere empty show**. If someone **asks me, "What are your plans today?"**, and I reply, "**I'm going to a concert in the park**", behind my sentence are **feelings, associations, desires**. And it is because **computers** are **rule-based, unconscious machines** that **do not** (and probably **cannot**) have such **feelings** and **intentions**, and that **human language** and **thought** involves **more than mere rule-following**, that **artificial intelligence** will **never achieve true self-awareness**.

"I am happy"

PATRIARCHY

A key component of second-wave feminism is the idea that the inequality of women is embedded in the structure of society itself, which is moulded and maintained to serve patriarchal male interests.

 NAME KATE MILLET

 DATES 1934–2017

 NATIONALITY AMERICAN

 SCHOOL FEMINISM

 MAIN WORKS *SEXUAL POLITICS*

 KEY CONTRIBUTIONS POLITICAL PHILOSOPHY, ETHICS

SEXUAL POLITICS

A **patriarchy** is a **male-dominated society** or **organization** where **men are accorded more power and status than women**. In her seminal work **Sexual Politics**, American feminist writer and activist **Kate Millet** analysed the **patriarchal nature of Western society and culture**, showing that the **secondary status of women** was **not due to some inherent biological inferiority**, but to a **system of values perpetuated by and for male interests**. In other words, **inequality was cultural, not biological**.

PHALLOCENTRISM

Thus Millet argues that even such literary intellectual figures, often considered *revolutionary* for their part in **challenging sexual prudishness** and **hypocrisy**, are in many ways *reactionary* when it comes to **relations between the sexes**. In advancing a **predominantly male-centred view of the world**, they are also – as other feminist thinkers have termed it – *phallocentric* (a term itself originating with **psychoanalysis**), a world in which **woman's key role is still to enable male ambitions**.

LITERARY CHAUVINISM

In illustrating her point, Millet targeted **twentieth-century male literary icons** such as **Norman Mailer**, **D. H. Lawrence** and **Henry Miller**, noting for instance how **Mailer's female characters** are often the subject of **casual violence** and **brutalization**, while **Lawrence's championing of sexual liberation** nonetheless **leaves intact traditional sex roles**, as he focuses primarily on **male sexuality** and **gratification**. Millet is **especially scornful** of the father of psychoanalysis **Sigmund Freud**, who notoriously **dismissed female desire for increased status** and **rights** as an expression of "**penis envy**", an **alleged stage of childhood female development** during which they experience **anxiety at their lack of male genitalia**.

QUALIA

In an influential thought experiment, Thomas Nagel argued that there are greater problems for explaining the nature of the mind than previous materialist philosophers had considered.

 NAME THOMAS NAGEL

 DATES 1937–

 NATIONALITY AMERICAN

 SCHOOL ANALYTIC PHILOSOPHY

 MAIN WORKS "WHAT IS IT LIKE TO BE A BAT?"; *MORTAL QUESTIONS; THE VIEW FROM NOWHERE*

 KEY CONTRIBUTIONS PHILOSOPHY OF MIND, ETHICS, METAPHYSICS

CONTEMPORARY PHILOSOPHY

BAT CONSCIOUSNESS

What is it like to be a bat? In asking this question, **Nagel** highlighted what at the time was a **little appreciated problem**. If we attempt to **imagine taking part in bat-like activity – flying around, eating insects** – the problem is that **bat eyesight** is **extremely limited**, and they **navigate** primarily by **echolocation** – emitting a **stream of clicks** and **measuring the time it takes the sound to bounce back from nearby objects**. But this is **so alien to any human experience** that, ultimately, we simply have to admit that we have **no idea what bat experience is like**.

QUALIA

These **elusive aspects of consciousness** have since become known as *qualia*: the **particular feelings** and **qualites** that **accompany perceptions**. Typical examples are **smells, colours, sensations** – things that are **hard to put into words**, and that are in some sense **private to each** individual. But if the **bat's** *qualia* are simply **unimaginable** to us, then doesn't that suggest that **mental** *qualia* themselves represent **aspects of consciousness** that **cannot be pinned down**, and which – **Nagel** implied – **no materialist philosophy can account for**?

PHENOMENAL CONSCIOUSNESS

Based on Nagel's insight, philosopher **David Chalmers** would later **divide consciousness** into **two types**: *psychological* and *phenomenal*. **Psychological consciousness** involves potentially **objective content (words, calculations**, etc.), and can arguably be **replicated on a computer**; **phenomenal content**, however, would always seem to **remain elusive** – not just that of **bats**, but of **humans** too.

LIBERTARIANISM

Libertarian philosopher Robert Nozick saw the duty of the state as involving the most minimal interference in the liberty of its citizens.

 NAME ROBERT NOZICK

 DATES 1938–2002

 NATIONALITY AMERICAN

 SCHOOL ANALYTIC PHILOSOPHY

 MAIN WORKS *ANARCHY, STATE AND UTOPIA; PHILOSOPHICAL EXPLANATIONS*

 KEY CONTRIBUTIONS POLITICAL PHILOSOPHY, EPISTEMOLOGY

MINARCHISM

In the terminology of **Isaiah Berlin** (discussed earlier), **libertarians** prioritize *negative freedom*: a **lack of state involvement**. Accordingly, if somewhat confusingly, a libertarian can be a **left-leaning** *anarchist*, believing in the *abolition* of **ownership, property** and the **state itself**; or a **right-wing** *minarchist*, seeing the **state's only legitimate role** as *guaranteeing* **ownership** and **natural rights**. We consider **anarchy** elsewhere, so let's look here at the **minarchism** of **Robert Nozick**.

DISTRIBUTIVE JUSTICE

Nozick's contemporary **John Rawls** asked how a **society** in which **some have more than they'll ever need** while **others lack even basic necessities** can ever be considered **fair**. He therefore **saw the state's duty** as **redistributing this wealth** in order to create **social justice**.

ENTITLEMENT THEORY

However, **Nozick questioned this**: if you build your **wealth** and **property** through **talent, hard work**, or **wise investment**, what **justifies** the **state** in **taxing you more** in order to **redistribute your wealth** to those who (perhaps) are *not* **as talented, hardworking**, or **prudent in their investments**? Shouldn't you be *entitled* to the **fruits of your labours**?

JUSTIFIED INEQUALITY

Nozick's **entitlement theory** therefore argues that **as long you've acquired, inherited**, or **bought** your property **justly** and **fairly**, then for the **state to take it away** from you would be an **infringement of your** *natural rights*. It may seem **unfair** that **some have more than others**, but, **as long as** everything was **done fairly and squarely**, this is no more "**unjust**" than the fact that I am **taller than you**, or you are a **faster runner** than I am.

taxman taxation

THE PLEASURE MACHINE

Robert Nozick rejected ethical hedonism, the idea that humans are only driven by pleasure and pain, because faced with a simulated reality of total bliss, we would reject it.

SIMULATED REALITY

To illustrate his point, **Nozick** asks us to consider a **choice**: to live in a **simulated reality** where **all our desires are met**, but to **know that it was false**; or to live an **ordinary life**, where **some or most of our desires are *not* met**, but we **know that everything we achieve is real**. Faced with this, Nozick argued, we would **reject the *pleasure machine***, because **happiness** and **fulfilment** are about **more than mere pleasure**.

RED AND BLUE PILLS

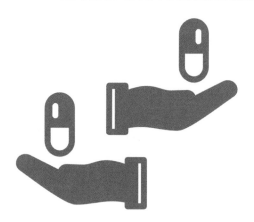

Anyone who has ever seen the film ***The Matrix*** will recognize here Neo's **choice** between the **blue** and **red pills**; between **simulated contentment** and **real but variable existence**. If you think that the choice is **easy**, and that you would **quickly get tired of artificial happiness**, you might also suppose that the **artificial reality** would be **indistinguishable from the real thing**. While choosing, you would **know the experience is going to be false**, but while **immersed** in it, your **achievements would feel genuine**.

MEANINGFUL EXPERIENCE

However, Nozick thinks you would still **choose reality**. As **Mill** argued, **humans don't just seek pleasure**, but **complex experiences** and **achievements** that are **pleasurable**. An **artist** doesn't just want **fame** or **money**, but **recognition** and **creative fulfilment**, which in turn may bring fame and money (or other forms of pleasure). And most fundamentally, we want to **develop as persons**, to acquire **admirable qualities** and **characteristics** (**persistence, ingenuity, compassion**) that **mean something to us**. These **may also give us pleasure**, but **without them**, pleasure **in itself** would be **empty** – just like the **simulated experiences** that produced them.

ZOMBIES

Daniel Dennett argues that there is no "hard problem" of consciousness, because the things that give rise to the problem – qualia – do not in fact exist.

 NAME DANIEL DENNETT

 DATES 1942–

 NATIONALITY AMERICAN

 SCHOOL ANALYTIC PHILOSOPHY

 MAIN WORKS *CONSCIOUSNESS EXPLAINED; DARWIN'S DANGEROUS IDEA*

 KEY CONTRIBUTIONS PHILOSOPHY OF MIND, PHILOSOPHY OF RELIGION

CARTESIAN THEATRE

Dennett criticizes what he terms the ***Cartesian theatre* view of the mind**. In this view, which he traces to **Descartes**, **mental experience** is imagined as if a **tiny version of ourselves sits before a screen** on which it **watches** our **sense experience**, **thoughts**, and **mental images**.

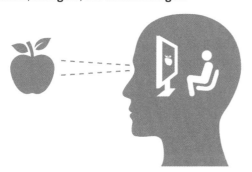

MULTIPLE DRAFTS

Instead, Dennett proposes what he calls the ***multiple drafts* theory** of **consciousness**. Rather than there being a **central place** where **consciousness exists**, he sees the **nervous system** as involved in a **constant process** of **scanning itself**, creating **multiple "drafts"** or "**stories**" that **constitute the self**. The self, then, is **not a "thing"** that **exists somewhere**, but rather a **process** – a sort of **narrative** that we are **continuously telling ourselves**.

THE HARD PROBLEM

The **"hard problem"** of **consciousness**, then – how **qualitative experiences** (***qualia***) can **arise** from **quantitative physical processes** – is therefore **just another part of this story**. As such, ***qualia* no more exist** than the **little man in our head** does.

philosophical zombie without *qualia*

person possessing *qualia*

PHILOSOPHICAL ZOMBIES

Arguing against this, philosophers such as **David Chalmers** have maintained that, **without *qualia***, a person would be **no more than a zombie**. Since such an idea is **incoherent**, there is **no possibility of such "philosophical zombies"** (people who walk and talk like us but who **possess no qualitative mental states**). **Dennett disagrees**: since *qualia* are an **illusion created by the nervous system, we are all** in effect "**zombies**".

HYPERREALITY

The concept of hyperreality is most often associated with French sociologist Jean Baudrillard, who argued that modern technology is making it impossible to distinguish the real from the false.

 NAME JEAN BAUDRILLARD

 DATES 1929–2007

 NATIONALITY FRENCH

 SCHOOL POST-STRUCTURALISM

 MAIN WORKS *SIMULACRA AND SIMULATION; THE GULF WAR DID NOT TAKE PLACE*

 KEY CONTRIBUTIONS EPISTEMOLOGY, AESTHETICS, METAPHYSICS

POST-STRUCTURALISM

Structuralism (discussed previously) was the view that a **culture must be understood** through its **underlying structure**, specifically as revealed through its **language**, **customs**, and **symbols**. However, **post-structuralists** – among whom **Baudrillard** may be classed – have, in various ways, **rebelled against this idea**.

HALL OF MIRRORS

Baudrillard's later philosophy takes this a step further. In a **consumerist, technological**, and **media-saturated society**, we increasingly live in a **world of signs**. As we move from **tin openers**, to **money**, to **designer clothing**, we **move further from what is real**, until ultimately **"reality" disappears**, hidden beneath the **world of signs** and their **values** that **we have created**. This is the *hyperreal*, a

SIGN EXCHANGE VALUE

Baudrillard was originally influenced by **Marx**, for whom a thing had a **use value**. A tin opener is useful for opening tins, and **valued accordingly**. Under **capitalism**, a thing is **worth what it can be exchanged for in the marketplace**. **Money** has **little value in itself** (as paper or metal), but **can be exchanged** for **food**, **clothes**, or other things with use value. Baudrillard takes this a step further, arguing that in a **modern consumerist society**, things are valued for their *sign exchange value*, as expressions of **status**, **sophistication**, and **taste**. In addition to its **price tag**, and **ability to keep us warm**, a piece of **designer clothing informs others** – in some indefinable way – of our **position in the social pecking order**.

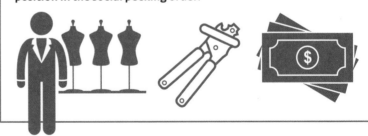

hall of mirrors where there are only **reflections**, and **no originals**, and where the **distinction** between "**real**" and "**artificial**", "**true**" and "**false**", ultimately **disappears**.

THE TELETRANSPORTER

In a famous thought experiment, Derek Parfit argued that psychological continuity was insufficient for personal identity.

 NAME DEREK PARFIT

 DATES 1942–2017

 NATIONALITY ENGLISH

 SCHOOL ANALYTIC PHILOSOPHY

 MAIN WORKS *REASONS AND PERSONS; ON WHAT MATTERS*

 KEY CONTRIBUTIONS PHILOSOPHY OF MIND, ETHICS

PSYCHOLOGICAL CONNECTEDNESS

Parfit agreed with **Locke** that it is the possession of the **same memories** and **personality traits** that makes someone the **same person over time**. However, while such *psychological connectedness* – the **overlapping connection** of such **memories** and **experiences** – may make "**future me**" the **same person as I am now**, there are **possible scenarios** where such a person **may not be** *uniquely* me.

RELATION R

Since "being you" is generally taken to imply **uniqueness**, and the transporter would create **two of "you"**, then Parfit's argument may be taken to show that – if we are just certain **configurations of physical atoms** – there can be **no such thing as personal identity**. All we have is the continued existence of what Parfit called "**Relation R**", which is a certain **configuration** of **memories** and **experiences** that persist through their **underlying physical properties**.

ATOMIC DUPLICATION

Imagine, he says, there's a teletransporter that can scan the **configuration of your atoms** and beam that information to Mars, where "you" are **reassembled** from Martian atoms. Would that person be "you"? It would have the **same memories** (possessing the **same physical brain states**), and your body would be **identical in organizational terms**, down to each follicle and freckle.

MIND UPLOADING

Similar **thought experiments** are common to **science fiction**. The transhumanist's hope that we will one day be able to **copy and upload minds onto computers** implies similar "**duplication**". But should such a thing ever become possible, this will create all sorts of problems – not just for **personal identity**, but also for **morality**, **law**, and almost **every aspect of social life**.

THE NON-IDENTITY PROBLEM

Philosophers continue to struggle with the obligations that we owe to future individuals who do not yet possess an identity, for it would seem better to exist than not, in whatever circumstances.

A UTILITARIAN CALCULATION

The problem, as independently identified by **Derek Parfit**, **Robert M. Adams**, and **Thomas Schwartz**, is that even a **life barely worthy living** is still **better than none at all**. It seems a strange decision to have to make, but would you rather **never have been born**, or live a life that, although hard and miserable at times, is still **just about worth living**? "As long as it's worth living," you might say, "then I choose to live!"

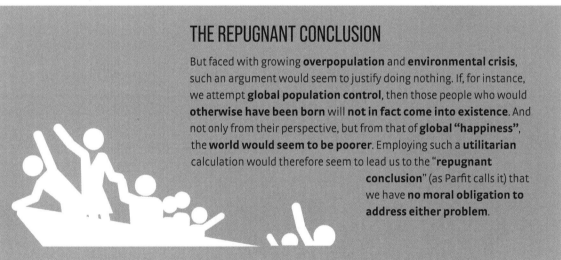

THE REPUGNANT CONCLUSION

But faced with growing **overpopulation** and **environmental crisis**, such an argument would seem to justify doing nothing. If, for instance, we attempt **global population control**, then those people who would **otherwise have been born** will **not in fact come into existence**. And not only from their perspective, but from that of **global "happiness"**, the **world would seem to be poorer**. Employing such a **utilitarian** calculation would therefore seem to lead us to the "**repugnant conclusion**" (as Parfit calls it) that we have **no moral obligation to address either problem**.

THE PERSON-AFFECTING VIEW

The answer here, as certain philosophers argue, is to **not construe morality in terms of actions being "good or bad for someone"**. If you remember **Mill's *principle of harm***, discussed earlier, then the very **basis of morality** is whether an **action is or is not bad for someone else**. If we give up the notion that our actions can **benefit** or **harm unborn people**, then perhaps we can **redress overpopulation and climate change with a clear conscience**. Another option would be to abandon the utilitarian calculation that makes that future person's life just about worth living. But either option comes with problems.

ELIMINATIVE MATERIALISM

Eliminative materialism argues that scientific understanding of the brain will eventually replace the very concepts we use to describe mental states.

 NAME PAUL CHURCHLAND

 DATES 1942–

 NATIONALITY AMERICAN

 SCHOOL ANALYTIC PHILOSOPHY

 MAIN WORKS "ELIMINATIVE MATERIALISM AND THE PROPOSITIONAL ATTITUDES"; *THE ENGINE OF REASON, THE SEAT OF THE SOUL*

 KEY CONTRIBUTIONS PHILOSOPHY OF MIND, EPISTEMOLOGY

SCIENTIFIC PROGRESS

The **progress of science** has seen us **"eliminate" numerous concepts and explanations** that were **once respectable** and **widely held**, but proved to be **baseless** or **unnecessary**. An example of this would be the *luminiferous ether*, a substance **once thought to pervade space** and **necessary** in order **to act as a medium through which light could travel**. But with **Einstein's new conception of *spacetime***, the ether could be **discarded**.

FOLK PSYCHOLOGY

In a similar way, philosophers such as **Paul** and **Patricia Churchland**, and **Daniel Dennett** have argued that **everyday notions** such as **"belief"**, **"desire"**, **"fear"**, and so on, are concepts that will also one day be **replaced** by more **robust scientific equivalents**. Such common notions are a form of **"folk psychology"**, they argue, resulting from **popular**, **naive**, and **ultimately mistaken ideas** of **what the mind is** and **how it works**.

THEORIES

This is of course a radical view. It's true that **many people hold wrong opinions about the world**, but **does this extend** to the **very concepts we use** to **describe our own and others' behaviour**, our **beliefs** and **desires**? John Searle argues that **everyday psychological language** isn't in fact **"theoretical"**. When I say, **"I'm in pain"**, I'm **not proposing a theory** that may be **proved wrong**; I'm **expressing how I feel** so that people will **help me**. Furthermore, I **might be mistaken** as to **where** or **why** a certain pain exists, but **not that I feel it**.

PORNOGRAPHY

The modern liberalization of attitudes towards sex in many countries has brought with it a greater focus on the question of whether pornography can ever be ethical.

 NAME CATHARINE A. MACKINNON

 DATES 1946–

NATIONALITY AMERICAN

 SCHOOL FEMINISM

 MAIN WORKS *FEMINISM UNMODIFIED; TOWARD A FEMINIST THEORY OF THE STATE*

 KEY CONTRIBUTIONS ETHICS, POLITICAL PHILOSOPHY

SEXUAL EXPLOITATION

A historical survey of what various cultures have considered "**pornographic**" reveals radically **differing** and **shifting attitudes** to **sex** and **propriety**. However, from certain **radical feminist perspectives**, the **same liberal forces that have fostered female emancipation** have ironically also given a **legal** and **cultural green light** to the **sexual degradation** and **exploitation** of **women**. Furthermore, with the advent of the **internet** and new forms of **media technology**, such portrayals are now **widely** and **easily accessible**, rendering them **almost impossible to police**.

CIVIL RIGHTS

The **increasing importance of this issue for feminism** was highlighted by American legal scholar **Catharine MacKinnon**, who, together with activist **Andrea Dworkin**, argued that **pornography should be considered a violation of civil rights** in that it **routinely involves** the infliction of **pain** and **humiliation**, **violence**, and **general degradation of women**. What's more, the **commercial incentives** to **producing pornography** often lead to other **illegal acts**, such as **people trafficking** and **sexual abuse**.

PRO-SEX FEMINISM

Against this, certain **third-wave feminists** have argued that **what is needed** is **not legislation** that **forces pornography back underground**, but an **open** and **evolving debate**. We must **balance concerns regarding abuse** and **exploitation** with recognition that **"pornography" may even form a legitimate** and **healthy part of female sexuality**. American journalist and activist **Ellen Willis** (1941–2006), who originated the term "**pro-sex feminism**", argued that such views as MacKinnon's and Dworkin's reinforce the **negative idea that women are passive victims of male sexual desire**, rather than **active participants with desires of their own**.

SPECIESISM

As a utilitarian, Peter Singer developed Bentham's view that animal rights should be based on their ability to suffer, and that any discrimination against them was in fact a form of speciesism.

 NAME PETER SINGER

 DATES 1946–

 NATIONALITY AMERICAN

 SCHOOL ANALYTIC PHILOSOPHY

 MAIN WORKS *ANIMAL LIBERATION; PRACTICAL ETHICS; THE LIFE YOU CAN SAVE*

 KEY CONTRIBUTIONS ETHICS, ANIMAL RIGHTS

DISCRIMINATION

Peter Singer argued that, just as we **should not treat someone differently** based on their **sex** or **race**, we **should not discriminate against animals** simply because they **are not the same species as us**. This is a radical argument that **puts animals** on an **equal moral footing with humans**, and one that considers the assertion that **animals do not possess the faculty of reason** as **irrelevan**t.

Sex   Race   Species

ETHICAL VEGANISM

Holding such a position would seem to **commit us** to **ethical veganism**, or the notion that **animals should not be exploited** for **food, clothing, medical experimentation**, or **entertainment**. However, the position **does not commit us** to the idea that animals should be treated *the same* as humans. Species **differ in their needs**: what would be **unethical treatment** of a **human** (deliberately **depriving them** of **clothing** or **shelter**) **might not apply** for instance to a **horse** or a **cow**.

MORAL DUTIES

Of course, many **non-utilitarian philosophers do not share these views**. For instance, English philosopher **Roger Scruton** argues that, since many animals are **incapable of behaving "morally"**, and would **gladly use humans as food**, then we have no **obligation to treat them as moral equals** because they are **incapable of fulfilling their moral duties to us**. This also **justifies us** in **using them as we wish**. Of course, this then opens the issue of **whether this should also apply** to human **"law breakers"**.

EFFECTIVE ALTRUISM

Associated with Peter Singer and William MacAskill (b.1987), effective altruism argues that we have a duty to give as much as possible to charity in order to alleviate the most suffering.

STRATEGIC GIVING

Whereas **altruism** is **central** to most **moral conceptions** of being "a **good person**", ***effective altruism*** argues that **charitable giving** should **strategically favour** those **causes** that will have the **greatest impact** upon **global pain** and **suffering**.

CONSEQUENCES

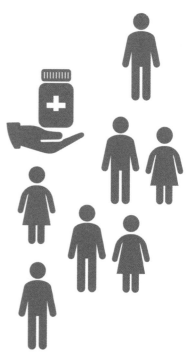

At the root of this is **Singer** and **MacAksill's utilitarianism**. For someone such as **Kant**, a **moral action** is **not to be judged by its consequences**, but by its **adherence** to the **moral law**. In such circumstances, giving to charity A is **no different** to giving to charity B (assuming both are **genuine charities**), for **both are good acts**. For **utilitarians**, however, as for other ***consequentialists***, this **ignores** the **amount of pain** and **deprivation** that a more **shrewd approach** would **alleviate**. Perhaps charity A is **better run** than B, or perhaps it **serves** a **greater** and **more pressing need**. As such, we should **favour that option**.

NEUTRALITY

Another consequence of this approach is that **charitable giving** should be **neutral** as to **causes**, **peoples**, and (in **Singer's case**) even **species**. It **should not matter which particular cause benefits**, **where those people live**, or even **whether they are human or animal**, but merely that **giving to it** has the **most benefit**. If, **relative to other causes**, your money most **benefits** the plight of **Antarctic penguins**, then Singer argues it **should be spent on that**, rather than the **homeless people in your neighbourhood**.

INCOME

How much, then, should you give? Singer argues that it should be **as much as you can afford** without putting yourself in an **equivalent state of suffering** – in his case, a **third of his salary**.

PANPSYCHISM

Given that qualitative mental properties represent a problem for the physicalist concept of mind, some philosophers have proposed that the physical universe as a whole possesses mental properties.

 NAME DAVID CHALMERS

 DATES 1966–

 NATIONALITY AUSTRALIAN

 SCHOOL ANALYTIC PHILOSOPHY

 MAIN WORKS *THE CONSCIOUS MIND*

 KEY CONTRIBUTIONS PHILOSOPHY OF MIND

ANIMISM

The idea that **consciousness** is **not just a property of humans** and **certain animals**, but **extends** into the **wider physical world**, is an **old one**. Many **early religions** were *animist*, assuming **consciousness** and **intention** in **rocks** and **trees**, as well as the **existence of free-roaming non-physical spirits**.

PHILOSOPHICAL EQUIVALENTS

However, ***panpsychism***, as this view is sometimes called, also has a **long philosophical tradition**, which can be traced from **Plato** to **Schopenhauer**, and, in modern times, to such thinkers as **Thomas Nagel**, **David Chalmers**, and – most recently – **Philip Goff**.

NON-EMERGENCE

A key feature of panpsychism is **non-emergence**. If **mental experiences** cannot be **reduced** to **purely physical properties**, or **explained away** as **illusory**, then we **must account for how they appear** to **"emerge"** from **inanimate matter**. But given the difficulties in doing this, what if such properties are ***non-emergent***, being **already somehow present in matter**? If **conscious experience** is **real**, and **"nothing can come from nothing"**, then **consciousness** must have a **pre-existing basis**.

MICRO AND MACRO

But does this mean that **fleas** are **conscious**, or **amoebae**, or perhaps even **rocks**? Australian philosopher **David Chalmers** argues that, while there is some sense in which they may be considered to have subjective **experiences**, such things as **bacteria** are only **conscious in a limited way** – they have what Chalmers calls ***micro-phenomenal consciousness***, whereas **human awareness** is ***macro-phenomenal***. By making this **distinction**, Chalmers **extends the definitions** of both **life** and **consciousness**, but in a way that attempts to **preserve our everyday assumption** that – in **human terms** – a **rock is still a rock**.

Micro-phenomenal consciousness ← → Macro-phenomenal consciousness

THE TROLLEY PROBLEM

In introducing the trolley problem, Philippa Foot formulated an ethical dilemma that highlighted a deep disagreement between different approaches to ethics.

 NAME PHILIPPA FOOT

 DATES 1920–2010

 NATIONALITY ENGLISH

 SCHOOL ANALYTIC PHILOSOPHY

 MAIN WORKS *VIRTUES AND VICES AND OTHER ESSAYS IN MORAL PHILOSOPHY; NATURAL GOODNESS*

 KEY CONTRIBUTIONS ETHICS, PHILOSOPHY OF MIND

THE DOCTRINE OF THE DOUBLE EFFECT

Foot discusses the **trolley problem** in relation to **abortion**, where she is concerned with the ***doctrine of double effect***: an **action** that **involves foreseen harm** is **permissible** *as long as that harm is not directly intended*. Where an **abortion saves a woman's life**, the **death of the foetus** is an **unavoidable** *indirect* consequence. It is the **intention**, not the **outcome**, that is **key**.

intended outcome   indirect but foreseen harm

SWITCHING TRACKS

Foot imagines a **runaway tram**. If the driver **maintains course**, **five men working on the track will die**; if he **switches**, **one man will die**. What should he do?

INTENTIONS AND OUTCOMES

The **dilemma** illustrates the difference between ***deontology*** and ***consequentialism***. The **deontologist** believes **taking life is always wrong**; by **switching tracks** the tram driver effectively *intends* that single person's death. Here, as with the **doctrine of double effect**, **intentions** are **important** in **deciding morality**. And yet, **isn't *not* acting also a decision**? The **consequentialist** will therefore argue against **double effect**: outcomes are more important than intentions. Weighing up the **consequences**, intended or not, it's **right to sacrifice one life to save five**.

COMPLICATIONS

Foot's **thought experiment** has recently taken on **new importance** in relation to the question of what "**moral system**" we should **programme into self-driving cars**. What is especially concerning is that, as a **survey of the ongoing debate** reveals, there would seem to be **no consensus** as to the **correct "solution"** to Foot's dilemma.

EPHIPHENOMENALISM

*One response to the problem of mind–body interaction is to assume that
our conscious mental experiences play no causal role.*

 NAME JAEGWON KIM

 DATES 1934–2019

 NATIONALITY KOREAN-AMERICAN

 SCHOOL ANALYTIC PHILOSOPHY

 MAIN WORKS *SUPERVENIENCE AND MIND; MIND IN A
PHYSICAL WORLD; PHYSICALISM, OR SOMETHING NEAR
ENOUGH*

 KEY CONTRIBUTIONS PHILOSOPHY OF MIND, METAPHYSICS,
EPISTEMOLOGY

THE PHYSICALIST'S DILEMMA

According to philosopher **Jaegwon Kim**, the **physicalist faces a
dilemma**. Either **qualitative mental states** are **not real** (a position held
by **Daniel Dennett**), or else somehow their **reality must be accepted** as
a **mysterious fact** of **mental experience**.

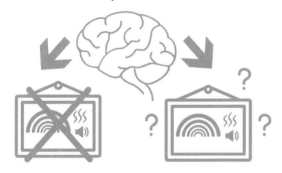

ILLUSORY CONTROL

Kim's **solution** is to argue for
a type of **epiphenomenalism**:
while the **physical brain causes
mental experience**, our **mental
reality** has **no causal power**.
This allows us to **treat the mind
scientifically** (**neurons influence
each other** through **physical
cause and effect**), but at the
expense of **mental control**: in
some **mysterious way**, **mental
events** are simply a **by-product**
of **physical processes**, giving only
the **illusion of control**.

TWO LANGUAGES

While he began by **defending** some version of **identity theory**, Kim
eventually **abandoned it**. The **language of brain states** is **not**, and will
never be, **equivalent** to that of **mental states**: "**this group of neurons is
firing**" can **never mean** the **same** thing as "**I think that car is nice, but far
too expensive**." The **two languages** are too **fundamentally different**. But if
we **give up** on trying to **translate mental states** into **physical brain states**,
and admit that **mental states** are in **some sense "real"**, this **undermines**
the **role played** by the **physical brain**: no matter what **physical neurons** do,
the **mind behaves according to its own rules** (**acting, choosing, liking,
feeling**) – and thus, we are back with **Cartesian dualism**.

GENDER

Modern feminists distinguish between sex, sexuality and gender, arguing that society imposes norms in an attempt to restrict behaviour and identity.

 NAME JUDITH BUTLER

 DATES 1956–

 NATIONALITY AMERICAN

 SCHOOL POSTMODERNISM/FEMINISM

 MAIN WORKS *GENDER TROUBLE; BODIES THAT MATTER*

 KEY CONTRIBUTIONS ETHICS, POLITICAL PHILOSOPHY, METAPHYSICS

NORMS

If we distinguish between **biological sex (male/female)**, **sexuality (sexual orientation)**, and **gender (masculinity/femininity)**, then the **traditional social norm** is for these to **correspond** – that a **woman should be heterosexual** and **feminine**, and a **man heterosexual** and **masculine**. These norms are frequently appealed to in order to **enforce conformity** and to **exclude** and **marginalize non-conformity**.

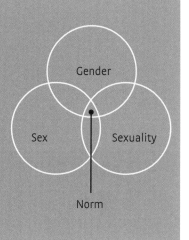

Gender

Sex   Sexuality

Norm

SEX AND BEHAVIOUR

In analysing things in this way, **second-wave feminists** such as **Gayle Rubin** (b.1949) sought to **push back against the notion** that a **person's sexuality**, **behaviour**, or **identity** should be **determined by their biological sex**. Rather, expectations of what is "**normal**" for a **woman** are **culturally, not naturally determined**, and **often fall in line with male-serving ideals**. Being a **good housewife** is **not written in the genes**.

PERFORMATIVITY

While agreeing that such differences are **socially determined**, American **third-wave** feminist philosopher **Judith Butler** pushes this further, arguing that ***all* such notions** – gender identity, sexuality, and biological sex – are ***performative***. By this she means that they are **culturally constructed "roles"** that we are **pressured to adopt** and **enact**. As such, Butler considers **all such distinctions** to have **no ultimate basis**, arguing that we possess not only **no essential gender identity**, but **no core identity at all** – it is all just **a show**, **a performance** – and even **biological sex** is merely an **arbitrary binary distinction** that is **no more than a "story"** we tell about the body that has evolved culturally through history.

TRANSHUMANISM

Transhumanism proposes that technology will allow humans not only to live longer, but to transcend what it means to be human.

 NAME NICK BOSTROM

 SCHOOL ANALYTIC PHILOSOPHY

 DATES 1973–

 MAIN WORKS "ARE YOU LIVING IN A COMPUTER SIMULATION?"; *SUPERINTELLIGENCE*

 NATIONALITY SWEDISH

 KEY CONTRIBUTIONS PHILOSOPHY OF MIND, ETHICS

AUGMENTATION

As well as **remedying genetic disorders** and **eradicating disease**, **technology**, transhumanists believe, will **extend human life** far beyond its **current limits**, even perhaps achieving a sort of **immortality** – through **biological means** (**genetic manipulation**, **regrowing** and **transplanting organs**, repairing cells with tiny "**nanobots**"), **technological implants** (**grafting artificial limbs**, augmenting mental and **physical capacities** by **implanting computer chips**), or purely **digital methods** (**scanning brains** and "**uploading**" **consciousness to a computer**).

THE SIMULATION HYPOTHESIS

This process will also bring **dangers**: **will these super-intelligent machines help us**, or **turn us into batteries**? Assuming we survive, Bostrom argues that, just as our **scientists** try to **visualize** the **lives of Neanderthal man**, future *posthumans* will use such **technology** to **run simulations** of what the **past was like**. But this technology will be **so powerful** as to allow them to **simulate consciousness itself**. In other words, the people **"living" in the simulation** would **feel they were "alive"**. And if this is possible, and technology seems **inevitably bound upon such a path of development**, can we know that we are **not *now* living in such a simulation**?

THE SINGULARITY

Such possibilities seem **far-fetched**, but transhumanists such as philosopher **Nick Bostrom** argue that, given **current trends** in **technological advance**, at least **some of these scenarios** are **likely to play out** – and perhaps **sooner than we think**. There will likely come a point where **computers can make smarter versions of themselves** – what's been termed the ***technological singularity***. This will create a process of **exponential growth**, where these **smarter computers** can create **even smarter computers** – and so on, **indefinitely**.

GLOSSARY

Anti-realism: the denial that our thoughts and perceptions correspond to an objective reality.

Behaviourism: the theory that mental processes can be explained in terms of actual or potential behaviour.

Circularity: an argument that relies in some way on the truth of what it seeks to prove.

Coherentism: the view that our beliefs are justified to the extent that they are coherent (fit) with our other beliefs.

Deduction: a form of argument where, if valid, and the premises are true, the conclusion is certain.

Deontology: the approach that sees ethics in terms of duty and obligation to moral rules or principles.

Determinism: the view that all actions are fixed and determined by some cause (e.g. physical, genetic, environmental).

Dialectic: a form of argument involving two opposing positions; in Hegel and Marx, the process of conflict that drives historical progress.

Dualism: the belief that there are two fundamental substances or principles; in philosophy of mind, the belief that mind is a separate substance from, or property of, the physical body.

Empiricism: the general approach that sees knowledge as ultimately justified by, and consisting of, sensory experience.

Enlightenment, Age of: a cultural period from the seventeenth to the nineteenth century stressing human rationality as the foundation of knowledge.

Epistemology: the branch of philosophy concerned with knowledge, what it is, and how it can be guaranteed.

Existentialism: a twentieth-century movement that emphasizes the role of individual subjective concerns in philosophical questions.

Foundationalism: the view in epistemology (e.g. Descartes) that argues that all knowledge must ultimately be based on undeniable truths.

Functionalism: the view in philosophy of mind that explains mental states in terms of the function they play.

Idealism: in metaphysics and epistemology, the general view that we do not perceive an independent reality, but only our own perceptions; in politics and international relations, the belief that foreign policy should reflect a state's internal political ideals (cf. realism).

Induction: a form of argument where the conclusion goes beyond the premises; uncertainty resulting from this produces the *problem of induction*.

Infinite regress: a faulty argument in which justification for each statement requires further justification (and so on infinitely).

Intentionality: a property of mental experiences that concerns what they are "about" (their subjective attitude or perspective).

Libertarianism: in metaphysics, this denotes the belief that we have free will; in political philosophy, the theory that advocates the maximum liberty of the individual and minimum state authority.

Liberty: the freedom of the individual in a political context.

Metaphysics: the branch of philosophy concerned with the ultimate nature of reality.

Monism: the view (e.g. Spinoza, Parmenides) that everything that exists is ultimately a single substance.

Moral realism: the view that moral judgements ultimately refer to real independent properties.

Natural philosophy: the early scientific theories of the Ancient Greek (pre-Socratic) philosophers;

another name for the natural sciences.

Natural rights: the view (e.g. Locke) that humans possess inherent rights independently of laws or convention.

Naturalism: the belief that the natural world is all that exists; in the field of ethics, that good is a natural property (e.g. pleasure).

Nihilism: the denial that life or the world has any inherent meaning or purpose.

Ontology: a branch of metaphysics concerned with the nature of Being and what ultimately exists.

Paradox: an apparently sound argument that nonetheless results in contradiction (e.g. Zeno).

Pessimism: the general belief (e.g. Schopenhauer) that human existence has overall a negative quality.

Phenomenology: a movement that approaches philosophical problems in terms of our subjective experience of the world.

Physicalism: the belief that only physical matter exists; in philosophy of mind, that the mind is just the physical brain.

Postmodernism: a general movement of (especially) Continental philosophers that questions the possibility of truth and objectivity.

Qualia: the subjective aspects of mental experience (e.g. smells, colours); also called "phenomenal consciousness".

Rationalism: the general approach that sees knowledge as ultimately justified by, and consisting of, rational ideas.

Realism: in political philosophy, specifically international relations, the belief that all nations act out of self-interest (cf. idealism). In epistemology and metaphysics, the conviction that a real world exists, independent of our beliefs.

Relativism: the view that "objective" truths or values are merely relative to something else.

Scepticism: the general approach that doubts and questions our justification for knowing something.

Solipsism: the belief that "only I exist".

Tautology: a statement that is necessarily true by virtue of its form (e.g. "A = A").

Teleological: having an inherent purpose, end, or design.

Theodicy: an attempt to justify God's nature and existence in the face of evil and suffering.

Totalitarianism: an oppressive form of government that limits individual freedom in service to the state.

Universals: the general property or idea that *particular* things possess or relate to (e.g. a red car).

Utilitarianism: the theory that moral actions maximize happiness (pleasure, preference) for the majority.

Virtue ethics: the moral theory that proposes that goodness and happiness stem from cultivating virtuous personal characteristics.

FURTHER READING

Philosophy texts can be quite intimidating. Here is a list of some of the more readable primary texts, together with some more engaging and lively secondary reading.

Primary Texts

The Last Days of Socrates, Plato

Existentialism and Humanism, Jean-Paul Sartre

Meditations on First Philosophy, René Descartes

The Prince, Niccolò Machiavelli

The Dao De Ching, Lao Tse

Secondary Texts

A History of Western Philosophy, Bertrand Russell

The Problems of Philosophy, Bertrand Russell

Philosophy: The Basics, Nigel Warburton

At the Existentialist Café, Sarah Bakewell

How to Live: A Life of Montaigne, Sarah Bakewell

Think, Simon Blackburn

Aristotle's Way, Edith Hall

ACKNOWLEDGEMENTS

My thanks to all those involved in the production of this book: to my editor Slav Todorov and everyone at Welbeck for their exemplary work; to Chris Stone for his stoic patience, support, and guidance; to Nick Fawcett, for his meticulous copy editing and polite correction of my many transgressions (grammatical and factual); and to Dynamo Limited, for translating my often ill-thought-out suggestions into beautiful illustrations and designs – I hope I wasn't too much of a pain.